Monsieur Thomas by John Fletcher

John Fletcher was born in December, 1579 in Rye, Sussex. He was baptised on December 20th.

As can be imagined details of much of his life and career have not survived and, accordingly, only a very brief indication of his life and works can be given.

Young Fletcher appears at the very young age of eleven to have entered Corpus Christi College at Cambridge University in 1591. There are no records that he ever took a degree but there is some small evidence that he was being prepared for a career in the church.

However what is clear is that this was soon abandoned as he joined the stream of people who would leave University and decamp to the more bohemian life of commercial theatre in London.

The upbringing of the now teenage Fletcher and his seven siblings now passed to his paternal uncle, the poet and minor official Giles Fletcher. Giles, who had the patronage of the Earl of Essex may have been a liability rather than an advantage to the young Fletcher. With Essex involved in the failed rebellion against Elizabeth Giles was also tainted.

By 1606 John Fletcher appears to have equipped himself with the talents to become a playwright. Initially this appears to have been for the Children of the Queen's Revels, then performing at the Blackfriars Theatre.

Fletcher's early career was marked by one significant failure; The Faithful Shepherdess, his adaptation of Giovanni Battista Guarini's Il Pastor Fido, which was performed by the Blackfriars Children in 1608.

By 1609, however, he had found his stride. With his collaborator John Beaumont, he wrote Philaster, which became a hit for the King's Men and began a profitable association between Fletcher and that company. Philaster appears also to have begun a trend for tragicomedy.

By the middle of the 1610s, Fletcher's plays had achieved a popularity that rivalled Shakespeare's and cemented the pre-eminence of the King's Men in Jacobean London. After his frequent early collaborator John Beaumont's early death in 1616, Fletcher continued working, both singly and in collaboration, until his own death in 1625. By that time, he had produced, or had been credited with, close to fifty plays.

Index of Contents

DRAMATIS PERSONAE

MEN

Valentine, a Gentleman lately return'd from Travel, Brother to Alice
Monsieur Thomas, a Fellow-Traveller
Sebastian, his Father
Francis, Valentine's Son, in love with Cellide
Hylas, a general Lover
Sam, a Gentleman, his friend
Launcelot, Monsieur Thomas his Man
Michael, a Gentleman, Valentine's Neighbour
Three Physicians, and an Apothecary

WOMEN

Alice, Valentine's Sister
Cellide, beloved by Valentine, in Love with Francis
Mary, niece to Valentine and Alice, in Love with Monsieur Thomas
Dorothea, Sister to Monsieur Thomas

ACTUS PRIMUS

SCÆNA PRIMA

Enter **ALICE** and **VALENTINE**.

ALICE
How dearly welcome you are!

VALENTINE
I know it,
And my best Sister, you are as dear to my sight,
And pray let this confirm it: how you have govern'd
My poor state in my absence, how my servants,
I dare, and must believe, else I should wrong ye,
The best and worthiest.

ALICE
As my womans wit, Sir,
Which is but weak and crazie.

VALENTINE
But good Alice,
Tell me how fares the gentle Cellide,
The life of my affection, since my travel,
My long and lazie Travel? is her love still
Upon the growing hand? does it not stop
And wither at my years? has she not view'd
And entertain'd some younger smooth behaviour,
Some Youth but in his blossom, as her self is?
There lies my fears.

ALICE
They need not, for believe me
So well you have manag'd her, and won her mind,
Even from her hours of childhood, to this ripeness,
And in your absence, that by me enforc'd still,
So well distill'd your gentleness into her,
Observ'd her, fed her fancy, liv'd still in her,
And though Love be a Boy, and ever youthful,
And young and beauteous objects ever aim'd at,
Yet here ye have gone beyond love, better'd nature,
Made him appear in years, in grey years fiery,
His Bow at full bent ever; fear not Brother,

For though your body has been far off from her,
Yet every hour your heart, which is your goodness,
I have forc'd into her, won a place prepar'd too,
And willingly to give it ever harbour;
Believe she is so much yours, and won by miracle,
(Which is by age) so deep a stamp set on her
By your observances, she cannot alter.
Were the Child living now ye lost at Sea
Among the Genoua Gallies, what a happiness!
What a main Blessing!

VALENTINE
O no more, good Sister,
Touch no more that string, 'tis too harsh and jarring.
With that Child all my hopes went, and you know
The root of all those hopes, the Mother too
Within few days.

ALICE
'Tis too true, and too fatal,
But peace be with their souls.

VALENTINE
For her loss
I hope the beauteous Cellide.

ALICE
You may, Sir,
For all she is, is yours.

VALENTINE
For the poor Boys loss,
I have brought a noble friend, I found in Travel,
A worthier mind, and a more temperate spirit,
If I have so much judgment to discern 'em,
Man yet was never master of.

ALICE
What is he?

VALENTINE
A Gentleman, I do assure my self,
And of a worthy breeding, though he hide it;
I found him at Valentia, poor and needy,
Only his mind the master of a Treasure.
I sought his friendship, won him by much violence,
His honesty and modesty still fearing
To thrust a charge upon me; how I love him,

He shall now know, where want and he hereafter
Shall be no more Companions, use him nobly,
It is my will, good Sister, all I have
I make him free companion in, and partner,
But only—

ALICE
 I observe ye, hold your Right there,
Love and high Rule allows no Rivals, Brother,
He shall have fair regard, and all observance.

[Enter **HYLAS**.

HYLAS
You are welcome, noble Sir.

VALENTINE
What, Monsieur Hylas!
I'm glad to see your merry Body well yet.

HYLAS
'Faith y'are welcome home, what news beyond seas?

VALENTINE
None, but new men expected, such as you are,
To breed new admirations; 'Tis my Sister,
'Pray ye know her, Sir.

HYLAS
With all my heart; your leave Lady?

ALICE
You have it, Sir.

HYLAS
A shrewd smart touch, which does prognosticate
A Body keen and active, somewhat old,
But that's all one; age brings experience
And knowledge to dispatch: I must be better,
And nearer in my service, with your leave, Sir,
To this fair Lady.

VALENTINE
What, the old 'squire of Dames still!

HYLAS
Still the admirer of their goodness; with all my heart now,
I love a woman of her years, a pacer

That lays the bridle in her Neck, will travel
Forty, and somewhat fulsome is a fine dish.
These young Colts are too skittish.

[Enter **MARY**.

ALICE
My Cousin Mary
In all her joy, Sir, to congratulate
Your fair return.

VALENTINE
My loving and kind Cousin,
A thousand welcomes.

MARY
A thousand thanks to heaven, Sir,
For your safe voyage, and return.

VALENTINE
I thank ye;
But where's my Blessed Cellide? her slackness
In visitation.

MARY
Think not so, dear Uncle,
I left her on her knees, thanking the gods
With tears and prayers.

VALENTINE
Ye have given me too much comfort.

MARY
She will not be long from ye.

HYLAS
Your fair Cousin?

VALENTINE
It is so, and a bait you cannot balk Sir,
If your old rule reign in you, ye may know her:
A happy stock ye have, right worthy Lady,
The poorest of your servants vows his duty
And obliged faith.

MARY
O 'tis a kiss you would, Sir,
Take it, and tye your tongue up.

HYLAS
I am an Ass
I do perceive now, a blind Ass, a Blockhead;
For this is handsomness, this that that draws us
Body and Bones: Oh what a mounted forehead,
What eyes and lips, what every thing about her!
How like a Swan she swims her pace, and bears
Her silver Breasts! this is the Woman, she,
And only she, that I will so much honour
As to think worthy of my love, all older Idols
I heartily abhor, and give to Gunpowder,
And all Complexions besides hers, to Gypsies.

[Enter **FRANCIS** at one door, and **CELLIDE** at another.

VALENTINE
O my dear life, my better heart, all dangers,
Distresses in my travel, all misfortunes,
Had they been endless like the hours upon me,
In this kiss had been buried in oblivion;
How happy have ye made me, truly happy!

CELLIDE
My joy has so much over mastered me,
That in my tears for your return—

VALENTINE
O dearest;
My noble friend too! what a Blessedness
Have I about me now! how full my wishes
Are come again, a thousand hearty welcomes
I once more lay upon ye; all I have,
The fair and liberal use of all my servants
To be at your command, and all the uses
Of all within my power.

FRANCIS
Ye are too munificent,
Nor am I able to conceive those thanks, Sir.

VALENTINE
Ye wrong my tender love now, even my service,
Nothing accepted, nothing stuck between us
And our intire affections but this woman,
This I beseech ye friend.

FRANCIS

It is a jewel,
I do confess, would make a Thief, but never
Of him that's so much yours, and bound your servant,
That were a base ingratitude.

VALENTINE
Ye are noble,
'Pray be acquainted with her, keep your way, Sir,
My Cousin and my Sister.

ALICE
Ye are most welcome.

MARY
If any thing in our poor powers, fair Sir,
To render ye content, and liberal welcome
May but appear, command it.

ALICE
Ye shall find us
Happy in our performance.

FRANCIS
The poor Servant
Of both your goodnesses presents his service.

VALENTINE
Come, no more Complement; Custom has made it
Dull, old, and tedious; ye are once more welcome
As your own thoughts can make ye, and the same ever.
And so we'll in to ratifie it.

HYLAS
Hark ye, Valentine:
Is wild Oats yet come over?

VALENTINE
Yes, with me, Sir.

MARY
How does he bear himself?

VALENTINE
A great deal better;
Why do you blush? the Gentleman will do well.

MARY
I should be glad on't, Sir.

VALENTINE
How does his father?

HYLAS
As mad a worm as e'er he was.

VALENTINE
I lookt for't:
Shall we enjoy your Company?

HYLAS
I'll wait on ye:
Only a thought or two.

VALENTINE
We bar all prayers.

[Exeunt all but **HYLAS**.

HYLAS
This last Wench! I, this last wench was a fair one,
A dainty Wench, a right one; a Devil take it,
What do I ail? to have fifteen now in liking,
Enough a Man would think to stay my stomach?
But what's fifteen, or fifteen score to my thoughts?
And wherefore are mine Eyes made, and have lights,
But to encrease my Objects? This last Wench
Sticks plaguey close to me, a hundred pound
I were as close to her; If I lov'd now,
As many foolish men do, I should run mad.

SCÆNA SECUNDA

Enter old **SEBASTIAN** and **LAUNCELOT**.

SEBASTIAN
Sirrah, no more of your French shrugs I advise you.
If you be lowzie shift your self.

LAUNCELOT
May it please your Worship.

SEBASTIAN
Only to see my Son, my Son, good Launcelot;
Your Master and my Son; Body O me Sir,

No money, no more money, Monsieur Launcelot,
Not a Denier, sweet Signior; bring the Person,
The person of my Boy, my Boy Tom, Monsieur Thomas,
Or get you gone again, du gata whee, Sir;
Bassa mi cu, good Launcelot, valetote.
My Boy or nothing.

LAUNCELOT
Then to answer punctually.

SEBASTIAN
I say to th' purpose.

LAUNCELOT
Then I say to th' purpose,
Because your Worships vulgar Understanding
May meet me at the nearest; your Son, my Master,
Or Monsieur Thomas, (for so his Travel stiles him)
Through many foreign plots that Vertue meets with,
And dangers (I beseech ye give attention)
Is at the last arriv'd
To ask your (as the French man calls it sweetly)
Benediction de jour en jour.

SEBASTIAN
Sirrah, do not conjure me with your French furies.

LAUNCELOT
Che ditt' a vou, Monsieur.

SEBASTIAN
Che doga vou, Rascal;
Leave me your rotten language, and tell me plainly,
And quickly, Sirrah, lest I crack your French Crown,
What your good Master means; I have maintain'd
You and your Monsieur, as I take it, Launcelot,
These two years at your ditty vous, your jours.
Jour me no more, for not another penny
Shall pass my purse.

LAUNCELOT
Your Worship is erroneous,
For as I told you, your Son Tom, or Thomas,
My master and your Son is now arriv'd
To ask you, as our Language bears it nearest,
Your quotidian Blessing, and here he is in Person.

[Enter **THOMAS**.

SEBASTIAN

What, Tom! Boy, welcome with all my heart, Boy
Welcome, 'faith thou hast gladded me at soul, Boy,
Infinite glad I am, I have pray'd too, Thomas,
For you wild Thomas, Tom, I thank thee heartily
For coming home.

THOMAS

Sir, I do find your Prayers
Have much prevail'd above my sins.

SEBASTIAN

How's this?

THOMAS

Else certain I had perish'd with my rudeness,
Ere I had won my self to that discretion,
I hope you shall hereafter find.

SEBASTIAN

Humh, humh,
Discretion? is it come to that? the Boy's spoil'd.

THOMAS

Sirrah, you Rogue, look for't, for I will make thee
Ten times more miserable than thou thought'st thy self
Before thou travell'dst; thou hast told my Father,
I know it, and I find it, all my Rogueries
By meer way of prevention to undo me.

LAUNCELOT

Sir, as I speak eight languages, I only
Told him you came to ask his benediction,
De jour en jour.

THOMAS

But that I must be civil,
I would beat thee like a Dog. Sir, however
The Time I have mispent may make you doubtful,
Nay harden your belief 'gainst my Conversion.

SEBASTIAN

A pox o' travel, I say.

THOMAS

Yet dear Father
Your own experience in my after courses.

[Enter **DOROTHEA**.

SEBASTIAN
Prithee no more, 'tis scurvy; there's thy Sister
Undone without Redemption; he eats with picks,
Utterly spoil'd, his spirit baffled in him:
How have I sin'd that this affliction
Should light so heavy on me? I have no more Sons;
And this no more mine own, no spark of Nature
Allows him mine now, he's grown tame; my grand curse
Hang o'r his head that thus transform'd thee: travel?
I'll send my horse to travel next; we Monsieur.
Now will my most canonical dear Neighbours
Say I have found my Son, and rejoyce with me,
Because he has mew'd his mad tricks off: I know not,
But I am sure this Monsieur, this fine Gentleman
Will never be in my Books like mad Thomas,
I must go seek an Heir, for my inheritance
Must not turn Secretary; my name and quality
Has kept my Land three hundred years in madness,
And it slip now, may it sink.

[Exit.

THOMAS
Excellent Sister,
I am glad to see thee well; but where's thy father?

DOROTHEA
Gone discontent, it seems.

THOMAS
He did ill in it
As he does all; for I was uttering
A handsome Speech or two, I have been studying
E'r since I came from Paris: how glad to see thee!

DOROTHEA
I am gladder to see you, with more love too
I dare maintain it, than my Father's sorry
To see (as he supposes) your Conversion;
And I am sure he is vext, nay more, I know it,
He has pray'd against it mainly; but it appears, Sir,
You had rather blind him with that poor opinion
Than in your self correct it: dearest Brother,
Since there is in our uniform resemblance,
No more to make us two but our bare Sexes;

And since one happy Birth produc'd us hither,
Let one more happy mind.

THOMAS
It shall be, Sister,
For I can do it when I list; and yet, Wench,
Be mad too when I please; I have the trick on't:
Beware a Traveller.

DOROTHEA
Leave that trick too.

THOMAS
Not for the world: but where's my Mistress,
And prithee say how does she? I melt to see her,
And presently: I must away.

DOROTHEA
Then do so,
For o' my faith, she will not see you Brother.

THOMAS
Not see me? I'll—

DOROTHEA
Now you play your true self;
How would my father love this! I'll assure you
She will not see you; she has heard (and loudly)
The gambols that you plaid since your departure,
In every Town ye came, your several mischiefs,
Your rowses and your wenches; all your quarrels,
And the no-causes of 'em; these I take it
Although she love ye well, to modest ears,
To one that waited for your reformation,
To which end travel was propounded by her Uncle,
Must needs, and reason for it, be examined,
And by her modesty, and fear'd too light too,
To fyle with her affections; ye have lost her
For any thing I see, exil'd your self.

THOMAS
No more of that, sweet Doll, I will be civil.

DOROTHEA
But how long?

THOMAS
Would'st thou have me lose my Birth-right?

For yond old thing will disinherit me
If I grow too demure; good sweet Doll, prithee,
Prithee, dear Sister, let me see her.

DOROTHEA
No.

THOMAS
Nay, I beseech thee, by this light.

DOROTHEA
I, swagger.

THOMAS
Kiss me, and be my friend, we two were twins,
And shall we now grow strangers?

DOROTHEA
'Tis not my fault.

THOMAS
Well, there be other women, and remember
You, you were the cause of this; there be more lands too,
And better People in 'em, fare ye well,
And other loves; what shall become of me
And of my vanities, because they grieve ye?

DOROTHEA
Come hither, come, do you see that Cloud that flies there?
So light are you, and blown with every fancy:
Will ye but make me hope ye may be civil?
I know your Nature's sweet enough, and tender,
Not grated on, nor curb'd: do you love your Mistress?

THOMAS
He lies that says I do not.

DOROTHEA
Would ye see her?

THOMAS
If you please, for it must be so.

DOROTHEA
And appear to her
A thing to be belov'd?

THOMAS

Yes.

DOROTHEA
Change then
A little of your wildness into wisdom,
And put on a more smoothness;
I'll do the best I can to help ye, yet
I do protest she swore, and swore it deeply,
She would never see you more; where's your mans heart now?
What, do you faint at this?

THOMAS
She is a woman;
But him she entertains next for a servant,
I shall be bold to quarter.

DOROTHEA
No thought of fighting;
Go in, and there we'll talk more, be but rul'd,
And what lies in my power, ye shall be sure of.

[Exeunt.

SCÆNA TERTIA

Enter **ALICE** and **MARY**.

ALICE
He cannot be so wild still.

MARY
'Tis most certain,
I have now heard all, and all the truth.

ALICE
Grant all that;
Is he the first that has been giv'n a lost man,
And yet come fairly home? he is young and tender,
And fit for that impression your affections
Shall stamp upon him, age brings on discretion,
A year hence, these mad toys that now possess him
Will shew like Bugbears to him, shapes to fright him;
Marriage dissolves all these like mists.

MARY
They are grounded

Hereditary in him, from his father,
And to his grave they will haunt him.

ALICE
'Tis your fear
Which is a wise part in you; yet your love
However you may seem to lessen it
With these dislikes, and choak it with these errors,
Do what you can, will break out to excuse him,
Ye have him in your heart, and planted, Cousin,
From whence the power of reason, nor discretion
Can ever root him.

MARY
Planted in my heart, Aunt?
Believe it no, I never was so liberal;
What though he shew a so so comely fellow
Which we call pretty? or say it may be handsom?
What though his promises may stumble at
The power of goodness in him, sometimes use too?

ALICE
How willingly thy heart betrays thee, Cousin?
Cozen thy self no more; thou hast no more power
To leave off loving him than he that's thirsty
Has to abstain from drink standing before him;
His mind is not so monstrous for his shape,
If I have Eyes, I have not seen his better.
A handsome brown Complexion.

MARY
Reasonable,
Inclining to a tawney.

ALICE
Had I said so
You would have wish'd my tongue out; then his making.

MARY
Which may be mended; I have seen legs straighter,
And cleaner made.

ALICE
A body too.

MARY
Far neater,
And better set together.

ALICE
God forgive thee,
For against thy Conscience thou lyest stubbornly.

MARY
I grant 'tis neat enough.

ALICE
'Tis excellent,
And where the outward parts are fair and lovely,
(Which are but moulds o'th' mind) what must the soul be?
Put case youth has his swinge, and fiery Nature
Flames to mad uses many times.

MARY
All this
You only use to make me say I love him;
I do confess I do, but that my fondness
Should fling it self upon his desperate follies.

ALICE
I do not counsel that, see him reclaim'd first,
Which will not prove a miracle, yet Mary,
I am afraid 'twill vex thee horribly
To stay so long.

MARY
No, no Aunt, no, believe me.

ALICE
What was your dream to-night? for I observ'd ye
Hugging of me, with good dear sweet Tom.

MARY
Fye, Aunt,
Upon my Conscience.

ALICE
On my word 'tis true, Wench;
And then ye kiss'd me, Mary, more than once too,
And sigh'd, and O sweet Tom again; nay, do not blush,
Ye have it at the heart, Wench.

MARY
I'll be hang'd first,
But you must have your way.

[Enter **DOROTHEA**.

ALICE
And so will you too,
Or break down hedges for it. Dorothea,
The welcom'st woman living; how does thy Brother?
I hear he's turn'd a wondrous civil Gentleman
Since his short travel.

DOROTHEA
'Pray Heaven he make it good, Alice.

MARY
How do ye friend? I have a quarrel to ye,
Ye stole away and left my company.

DOROTHEA
O pardon me, dear friend, it was to welcome
A Brother that I have some Cause to love well.

MARY
Prithee how is he? thou speak'st truth.

DOROTHEA
Not perfect,
I hope he will be.

MARY
Never: h'as forgot me,
I hear Wench, and his hot love too.

ALICE
Thou would'st howl then.

MARY
And I am glad it should be so; his travels
Have yielded him variety of Mistresses,
Fairer in his eye far.

ALICE
O cogging Rascal!

MARY
I was a fool, but better thoughts I thank heaven.

DOROTHEA
'Pray do not think so, for he loves you dearly,
Upon my troth most firmly, would fain see you.

MARY
See me friend! do you think it fit?

DOROTHEA
It may be,
Without the loss of credit too; he's not
Such a prodigious thing, so monstrous,
To fling from all society.

MARY
He's so much contrary
To my desires, such an antipathy
That I must sooner see my grave.

DOROTHEA
Dear friend,
He was not so before he went.

MARY
I grant it,
For then I daily hop'd his fair Conversion.

ALICE
Come, do not mask your self, but see him freely,
Ye have a mind.

MARY
That mind I'll master then.

DOROTHEA
And is your hate so mortal?

MARY
Not to his person,
But to his qualities, his mad-cap follies,
Which still like Hydras heads grow thicker on him.
I have a credit, friend, and Maids of my sort,
Love where their modesties may live untainted.

DOROTHEA
I give up that hope then; 'pray for your friends sake,
If I have any interest within ye,
Do but this courtesie, accept this Letter.

MARY
From him?

DOROTHEA
The same; 'tis but a minutes reading,
And as we look on shapes of painted Devils,
Which for the present may disturb our fancy,
But with the next new object lose 'em, so
If this be foul, ye may forget it, 'pray.

MARY
Have ye seen it, friend?

DOROTHEA
I will not lie; I have not,
But I presume, so much he honours you,
The worst part of himself was cast away
When to his best part he writ this.

MARY
For your sake,
Not that I any way shall like his scribling.

ALICE
A shrewd dissembling Quean.

DOROTHEA
I thank ye, dear friend,
I know she loves him.

ALICE
Yes, and will not lose him,
Unless he leap into the Moon, believe that,
And then she'l scramble too; young wenches loves
Are like the course of quartans, they may shift
And seem to cease sometimes, and yet we see
The least distemper pulls 'em back again,
And seats 'em in their old course; fear her not,
Unless he be a Devil.

MARY
Now Heaven bless me.

DOROTHEA
What has he writ?

MARY
Out, out upon him.

DOROTHEA
Ha, what has the mad man done?

MARY
Worse, worse, and worse still.

ALICE
Some Northern Toy, a little broad.

MARY
Still fouler!
Hey, hey Boys, goodness keep me; Oh.

DOROTHEA
What ail ye?

MARY
Here, take your Spell again, it burns my fingers.
Was ever Lover writ so sweet a Letter?
So elegant a style? pray look upon't;
The rarest inventory of rank Oaths
That ever Cut-purse cast.

ALICE
What a mad Boy is this!

MARY
Only i'th' bottom
A little Julip gently sprinkled over
To cool his mouth, lest it break out in blisters,
Indeed law. Yours for ever.

DOROTHEA
I am sorry.

MARY
You shall be welcome to me, come when you please,
And ever may command me vertuously,
But for your Brother, you must pardon me,
Till I am of his nature, no access friend,
No word of visitation, as ye love me,
And so for now I'le leave ye.

[Exit.

ALICE
What a letter
Has this thing written, how it roars like thunder!
With what a state he enters into stile!
Dear Mistress.

DOROTHEA
Out upon him bedlam.

ALICE
Well, there be waies to reach her yet: such likeness
As you two carry me thinks.

DOROTHEA
I am mad too,
And yet can apprehend ye: fare ye well,
The fool shall now fish for himself.

ALICE
Be sure then
His tewgh be tith and strong: and next no swearing,
He'l catch no fish else, Farewel Dol.

DOROTHEA
Farewel Alice

[Exeunt.

ACTUS SECUNDUS

SCÆNA PRIMA

Enter **VALENTINE**, **ALICE** and **CELLIDE**.

CELLIDE
Indeed he's much chang'd, extreamly alter'd,
His colour faded strangely too.

VALENTINE
The air,
The sharp and nipping air of our new climate
I hope is all, which will as well restore
To health again th' affected body by it,
And make it stronger far, as leave it dangerous;
How do's my sweet, our blessed hour comes on now
Apace my Cellide, (it knocks at door)
In which our loves, and long desires like rivers
Rising asunder far, shall fall together,
Within these two daies dear.

CELLIDE
When heaven, and you Sir
Shall think it fit: for by your wills I am govern'd.

ALICE
'Twere good some preparation.

[Enter **FRANK**.

VALENTINE
All that may be:
It shall be no blind wedding: and all the joy
Of all our friends I hope: he looks worse hourly,
How does my friend, my self? he sweats too coldly,
His pulse, like the slow dropping of a spowt,
Scarce gives his function: how is't man, alas Sir,
You look extreme ill: is it any old grief,
The weight of which?

FRANCIS
None, gentle Sir, that I feel,
Your love is too too tender,
Nay believe Sir.

CELLIDE
You cannot be the master of your health,
Either some feaver lyes in wait to catch ye,
Whose harbinger's already in your face
We see preparing: or some discontent,
Which if it lye in this house, I dare say
Both for this noble Gentleman, and all
That live within it, shall as readily
Be purg'd away, and with as much care soften'd,
And where the cause is.

FRANCIS
'Tis a joy to be ill,
Where such a vertuous fair Physitian
Is ready to relieve: your noble cares
I must, and ever shall be thankfull for,
And would my service (I dare not look upon her)
But be not fearfull, I feel nothing dangerous,
A grudging caus'd by th' alteration
Of air, may hang upon me: my heart's whole,
(I would it were.)

VALENTINE
I knew the cause to be so.

FRANCIS
No, you shall never know it.

ALICE
Some warm broths
To purge the bloud, and keep your bed a day Sir,
And sweat it out.

CELLIDE
I have such cordials,
That if you will but promise me to take 'em,
Indeed you shall be well, and very quickly,
I'le be your Doctor, you shall see how finely
I'le fetch ye up again.

VALENTINE
He sweats extreamly:
Hot, very hot: his pulse beats like a drum now,
Feel Sister, feel, feel sweet.

FRANCIS
How that touch stung me!

VALENTINE
My gown there.

CELLIDE
And those julips in the window.

ALICE
Some see his bed made.

VALENTINE
This is most unhappy,
Take courage man, 'tis nothing but an ague.

CELLIDE
And this shall be the last fit.

FRANCIS
Not by thousands:
Now what 'tis to be truly miserable,
I feel at full experience.

ALICE
He grows fainter.

VALENTINE
Come, lead him in, he shall to bed: a vomit,
I'le have a vomit for him.

ALICE
A purge first,
And if he breath'd a vein.

VALENTINE
No, no, no bleeding,
A Clyster will cool all.

CELLIDE
Be of good cheer Sir.

ALICE
He's loth to speak.

CELLIDE
How hard he holds my hand aunt!

ALICE
I do not like that sign.

VALENTINE
Away to's chamber,
Softly, he's full of pain, be diligent
With all the care ye have: would I had scus'd him.

[Exeunt.

SCÆNA SECUNDA

Enter **DOROTHEA** and **THOMAS**.

DOROTHEA
Why do you rail at me? do I dwell in her
To force her to do this or that? your letter,
A wilde-fire on your letter; your sweet Letter;
You are so learned in your writs: ye stand now
As if ye had worried sheep: you must turn tippet,
And suddenly, and truely, and discreetly
Put on the shape of order and humanity,
Or you must marry Malkyn the May Lady:
You must, dear Brother: do you make me carrier
Of your confound-mee's, and your culverings?

Am I a seemly agent for your oaths?
Who would have writ such a debosh'd?

THOMAS
Your patience,
May not a man profess his love?

DOROTHEA
In blasphemies?
Rack a maids tender ears, with dam's and Devils?

THOMAS
Out, out upon thee,
How would you have me write?
Begin with my love premised? surely,
And by my truly Mistress.

DOROTHEA
Take your own course,
For I see all perswasion's lost upon ye:
Humanitie, all drown'd: from this hour fairly
I'le wash my hands of all ye do: farewel Sir.

THOMAS
Thou art not mad?

DOROTHEA
No, if I were, dear Brother
I would keep you company: get a new Mistress
Some suburb Saint, that six pence, and some others
Will draw to parley: carowse her health in Cans
And candles ends, and quarrel for her beauty,
Such a sweet heart must serve your turn: your old love
Releases ye of all your tyes; disclaims ye
And utterly abjures your memory
Till time has better manag'd ye, will ye command me—

THOMAS
What, bob'd of all sides?

DOROTHEA
Any worthy service
Unto my Father Sir, that I may tell him
Even to his peace of heart, and much rejoycing
Ye are his true Son Tom still? will it please ye
To beat some half a dozen of his servants presently,
That I may testifie you have brought the same faith
Unblemish'd home, ye carried out? or if it like you

There be two chambermaids within, young wenches,
Handsom and apt for exercise: you have been good, Sir,
And charitable though I say it Signiour
To such poor orphans: and now, by th' way I think on't
Your young rear Admiral, I mean your last bastard
Don John, ye had by Lady Blanch the Dairy Maid,
Is by an Academy of learned Gypsies,
Foreseeing some strange wonder in the infant
Stoln from the Nurse, and wanders with those Prophets.
There is plate in the parlour, and good store Sir,
When your wants shall supply it. So most humbly
(First rendring my due service) I take leave Sir.

[Exit.

THOMAS
Why Doll, why Doll I say: my letter fub'd too,
And no access without I mend my manners?
All my designes in Limbo? I will have her,
Yes, I will have her, though the Devil roar,
I am resolv'd that, if she live above ground,
I'le not be bob'd i'th' nose with every bobtail:
I will be civil too, now I think better,
Exceeding civil, wondrous finely carried:
And yet be mad upon occasion,
And stark mad too, and save my land: my Father,
I'le have my will of him, how e're my wench goes.

[Exit.

[Enter **SEBASTIAN** and **LAUNCELOT**.

SEBASTIAN
Sirrah, I say still you have spoil'd your Master: leave your stiches:
I say thou hast spoil'd thy Master.

LAUNCELOT
I say how Sir?

SEBASTIAN
Marry thou hast taught him like an arrant rascal,
First to read perfectly: which on my blessing
I warn'd him from: for I knew if he read once,
He was a lost man. Secondly, Sir Launcelot,
Sir lowsie Launcelot, ye have suffer'd him
Against my power first, then against my precept,
To keep that simpring sort of people company,

That sober men call civil: mark ye that Sir?

LAUNCELOT
And't please your worship.

SEBASTIAN
It does not please my worship,
Nor shall not please my worship: thirdly and lastly,
Which if the law were here, I would hang thee for,
(However I will lame thee) like a villain,
Thou hast wrought him
Clean to forget what 'tis to do a mischief,
A handsom mischief, such as thou knew'st I lov'd well.
My servants all are sound now, my drink sowr'd,
Not a horse pawn'd, nor plaid away: no warrants
Come for the breach of peace.
Men travel with their mony, and nothing meets 'em:
I was accurs'd to send thee, thou wert ever
Leaning to laziness, and loss of spirit,
Thou slept'st still like a cork upon the water.

LAUNCELOT
Your worship knows, I ever was accounted
The most debosh'd, and please you to remember,
Every day drunk too, for your worships credit,
I broke the Butlers head too.

SEBASTIAN
No, base Palliard,
I do remember yet that anslaight, thou wast beaten,
And fledst before the Butler; a black jack
Playing upon thee furiously, I saw it:
I saw thee scatter'd rogue, behold thy Master.

[Enter **THOMAS** with a Book.

THOMAS
What sweet content dwells here!

LAUNCELOT
Put up your Book Sir,
We are all undone else.

SEBASTIAN
Tom, when is the horse-race?

THOMAS
I know not Sir.

SEBASTIAN
You will be there?

THOMAS
Not I Sir,
I have forgot those journeys.

SEBASTIAN
Spoil'd for ever.
The Cocking holds at Derby, and there will be
Jack Wild-oats, and Will Purser.

THOMAS
I am sorry, Sir,
They should employ their time so slenderly,
Their understandings will bear better courses.

SEBASTIAN
Yes, I will marry again: but Monsieur Thomas,
What say ye to the Gentleman that challeng'd ye
Before he went, and the fellow ye fell out with?

THOMAS
O good Sir,
Remember not those follies; where I have wrong'd, Sir,
(So much I have now learn'd to discern my self)
My means, and my repentance shall make even,
Nor do I think it any imputation
To let the Law perswade me.

SEBASTIAN
Any Woman:
I care not of what colour, or complexion,
Any that can bear Children: rest ye merry.

[Exit.

LAUNCELOT
Ye have utterly undone; clean discharg'd me,
I am for the ragged Regiment.

THOMAS
Eight languages,
And wither at an old mans words?

LAUNCELOT
O pardon me.

I know him but too well: eightscore I take it
Will not keep me from beating, if not killing:
I'le give him leave to break a leg, and thank him:
You might have sav'd all this, and sworn a little:
What had an oath or two been? or a head broke,
Though 'thad been mine, to have satisfied the old man?

THOMAS
I'le break it yet.

LAUNCELOT
Now 'tis too late, I take it:
Will ye be drunk to night, (a less intreaty
Has serv'd your turn) and save all yet? not mad drunk,
For then ye are the Devil, yet the drunker,
The better for your Father still: your state is desperate,
And with a desperate cure ye must recover it:
Do something, do Sir: do some drunken thing,
Some mad thing, or some any thing to help us.

THOMAS
Go for a Fidler then: the poor old Fidler
That sayes his Songs: but first where lyes my Mistris,
Did ye enquire out that?

LAUNCELOT
I'th' Lodge, alone Sir,
None but her own Attendants.

THOMAS
'Tis the happier:
Away then, find this Fidler, and do not miss me
By nine a Clock.

LAUNCELOT
Via.

[Exit.

THOMAS
My Father's mad now,
And ten to one will disinherit me:
I'le put him to his plunge, and yet be merry.
What Ribabald?

[Enter **HYLAS** and **SAM**.

HYLAS

Don Thomasio.
De bene venew.

THOMAS
I do embrace your body:
How do'st thou Sam?

SAM
The same Sam still: your friend Sir.

THOMAS
And how is't bouncing boyes?

HYLAS
Thou art not alter'd,
They said thou wert all Monsieur.

THOMAS
O believe it,
I am much alter'd, much another way:
The civil'st Gentleman in all your Country:
Do not ye see me alter'd? yea, and nay Gentlemen,
A much converted man: where's the best wine boyes?

HYLAS
A sound Convertite.

THOMAS
What, hast thou made up twenty yet?

HYLAS
By'r Lady,
I have giv'n a shrewd push at it, for as I take it,
The last I fell in love with, scor'd sixteen.

THOMAS
Look to your skin, Rambaldo the sleeping Gyant
Will rowze and rent thee piece-meal.

SAM
He ne'r perceives 'em
Longer than looking on.

THOMAS
Thou never meanest then
To marry any that thou lov'st?

HYLAS

No surely,
Nor any wise man I think; marriage?
Would you have me now begin to be prentice,
And learn to cobble other mens old Boots?

SAM
Why, you may take a Maid.

HYLAS
Where? can you tell me?
Or if 'twere possible I might get a Maid,
To what use should I put her? look upon her,
Dandle her upon my knee, and give her sugar-sops?
All the new Gowns i'th' Parish will not please her,
If she be high bred, for there's the sport she aims at,
Nor all the feathers in the Fryars.

THOMAS
Then take a Widow,
A good stanch wench, that's tith.

HYLAS
And begin a new order,
Live in a dead mans monument, not I, Sir,
I'll keep mine own road, a true mendicant;
What pleasure this day yields me, I never covet
To lay up for the morrow; and methinks ever
Anothers mans Cook dresses my diet neatest.

THOMAS
Thou wast wont to love old women, fat and flat nosed,
And thou would'st say they kiss'd like Flounders, flat
All the face over.

HYLAS
I have had such damsels
I must confess.

THOMAS
Thou hast been a precious Rogue.

SAM
Only his eyes; and o' my Conscience
They lye with half the Kingdom.

[Enter over the Stage, **PHYSICIANS** and others.

THOMAS

What's the matter?
Whither go all these men-menders, these Physicians?
Whose Dog lies sick o'th' mulligrubs?

SAM
O the Gentleman,
The young smug Seigniour, Master Valentine,
Brought out of travel with him, as I hear,
Is faln sick o'th' sudden, desperate sick,
And likely they go thither.

THOMAS
Who? young Frank?
The only temper'd spirit, Scholar, Souldier,
Courtier; and all in one piece? 'tis not possible.

[Enter **ALICE**.

SAM
There's one can better satisfie you.

THOMAS
Mistress Alice,
I joy to see you, Lady.

ALICE
Good Monsieur Thomas,
You're welcome from your travel; I am hasty,
A Gentleman lyes sick, Sir.

THOMAS
And how dost thou?
I must know, and I will know.

ALICE
Excellent well,
As well as may be, thank ye.

THOMAS
I am glad on't,
And prithee hark.

ALICE
I cannot stay.

THOMAS
A while, Alice.

SAM
Never look so narrowly, the mark's in her mouth still.

HYLAS
I am looking at her legs, prithee be quiet.

ALICE
I cannot stay.

THOMAS
O sweet Alice.

HYLAS
A clean instep,
And that I love a life, I did not mark
This woman half so well before, how quick
And nimble like a shadow, there her leg shew'd;
By th'mass a neat one, the colour of her Stocking,
A much inviting colour.

ALICE
My good Monsieur,
I have no time to talk now.

HYLAS
Pretty Breeches,
Finely becoming too.

THOMAS
By Heaven.

ALICE
She will not,
I can assure you that, and so.

THOMAS
But this word.

ALICE
I cannot, nor I will not, good Lord.

[Exit.

HYLAS
Well, you shall hear more from me.

THOMAS
We'll go visit,

'Tis Charity; besides, I know she is there;
And under visitation I shall see her;
Will ye along?

HYLAS
By any means.

THOMAS
Be sure then
I be a civil man: I have sport in hand, Boys,
Shall make mirth for a Marriage-day.

HYLAS
Away then.

[Exeunt.

SCÆNA TERTIA

Enter three **PHYSICIANS** with an Urinal.

1ST PHYSICIAN
A Pleurisie, I see it.

2ND PHYSICIAN
I rather hold it
For tremor Cordis.

3RD PHYSICIAN
Do you mark the Fæces?
'Tis a most pestilent contagious Feaver,
A surfeit, a plaguey surfeit; he must bleed.

1ST PHYSICIAN
By no means.

3RD PHYSICIAN
I say bleed.

1ST PHYSICIAN
I say 'tis dangerous;
The Person being spent so much before-hand,
And Nature drawn so low, Clysters, cool Clysters.

2ND PHYSICIAN
Now with your favours I should think a Vomit:

For take away the Cause, the Effect must follow,
The Stomach's foul and fur'd, the pot's unflam'd yet.

3RD PHYSICIAN
No, no, we'll rectifie that part by mild means,
Nature so sunk must find no violence.

[Enter a **SERVANT**.

SERVANT
Will't please ye draw near? the weak Gentleman
Grows worse and worse still.

1ST PHYSICIAN
Come, we will attend him.

2ND PHYSICIAN
He shall do well, my friend.

SERVANT
My Masters love, Sir.

1ST PHYSICIAN
Excellent well I warrant thee, right and straight, friend.

3RD PHYSICIAN
There's no doubt in him, none at all, ne'r fear him.

[Exeunt.

SCÆNA QUARTA

Enter **VALENTINE** and **MICHAEL**.

MICHAEL
That he is desperate sick I do believe well,
And that without a speedy cure it kills him,
But that it lyes within the help of Physick
Now to restore his health, or art to cure him;
Believe it you are cozen'd; clean beside it.
I would tell ye the true cause too, but 'twould vex ye,
Nay, run ye mad.

VALENTINE
May all I have restore him!
So dearly and so tenderly I love him,

I do not know the cause why, yea my life too.

MICHAEL
Now I perceive ye so well set, I'll tell you,
Hei mihi quod nullis Amor est medicabilis herbis.

VALENTINE
'Twas that I only fear'd: good friend go from me,
I find my heart too full for further conference;
You are assur'd of this?

MICHAEL
'Twill prove too certain,
But bear it nobly, Sir, Youth hath his errours.

VALENTINE
I shall do, and I thank ye; 'pray ye no words on't.

MICHAEL
I do not use to talk, Sir.

[Exit.

VALENTINE
Ye are welcome;
Is there no Constancy in earthly things,
No happiness in us, but what must alter?
No life without the heavy load of Fortune?
What miseries we are, and to our selves,
Even then when full content seems to sit by us,
What daily sores and sorrows!

[Enter **ALICE**.

ALICE
O dear Brother,
The Gentleman if ever you will see him
Alive as I think.

[Enter **CELLIDE**.

CELLIDE
O he faints, for Heavens sake,
For Heavens sake, Sir.

VALENTINE
Go comfort him, dear Sister.

[Exit **ALICE**.

And one word, sweet, with you; then we'll go to him.
What think you of this Gentleman?

CELLIDE
My pity thinks, Sir,
'Tis great misfortune that he should thus perish.

VALENTINE
It is indeed, but Cellide, he must dye.

CELLIDE
That were a cruelty, when care may cure him,
Why do you weep so, Sir? he may recover.

VALENTINE
He may, but with much danger; my sweet Cellide,
You have a powerful tongue.

CELLIDE
To do you service.

VALENTINE
I will betray his grief; he loves a Gentlewoman,
A friend of yours, whose heart another holds,
He knows it too; yet such a sway blind fancy,
And his not daring to deliver it,
Have won upon him, that they must undo him:
Never so hopeful and so sweet a Spirit,
Misfortune fell so foul on.

CELLIDE
Sure she's hard hearted,
That can look on, and not relent, and deeply
At such a misery; she is not married?

VALENTINE
Not yet.

CELLIDE
Nor near it?

VALENTINE
When she please.

CELLIDE
And pray Sir,

Does he deserve her truly, that she loves so?

VALENTINE
His love may merit much, his Person little,
For there the match lyes mangled.

CELLIDE
Is he your friend?

VALENTINE
He should be, for he is near me.

CELLIDE
Will not he dye then,
When th'other shall recover?

VALENTINE
Ye have pos'd me.

CELLIDE
Methinks he should go near it, if he love her;
If she love him.

VALENTINE
She does, and would do equal.

CELLIDE
'Tis a hard task you put me; yet for your sake
I will speak to her, all the art I have;
My best endeavours; all his Youth and Person,
His mind more full of beauty; all his hopes
The memory of such a sad example,
Ill spoken of, and never old; the curses
Of loving maids, and what may be alledg'd
I'll lay before her: what's her Name? I am ready.

VALENTINE
But will you deal effectually?

CELLIDE
Most truly;
Nay, were it my self, at your entreaty.

VALENTINE
And could ye be so pitiful?

CELLIDE
So dutiful;

Because you urge it, Sir.

VALENTINE
It may be then
It is your self.

CELLIDE
It is indeed, I know it,
And now know how ye love me.

VALENTINE
O my dearest,
Let but your goodness judge; your own part's pity;
Set but your eyes on his afflictions;
He is mine, and so becomes your charge: but think
What ruine Nature suffers in this young man,
What loss humanity, and noble manhood;
Take to your better judgment my declining,
My Age hung full of impotence, and ills,
My Body budding now no more: seer Winter
Hath seal'd that sap up, at the best and happiest
I can but be your infant, you my Nurse,
And how unequal dearest; where his years,
His sweetness, and his ever spring of goodness,
My fortunes growing in him, and my self too,
Which makes him all your old love; misconceive not,
I say not this as weary of my bondage,
Or ready to infringe my faith; bear witness,
Those eyes that I adore still, those lamps that light me
To all the joy I have.

CELLIDE
You have said enough, Sir,
And more than e'r I thought that tongue could utter,
But you are a man, a false man too.

VALENTINE
Dear Cellide.

CELLIDE
And now, to shew you that I am a woman
Rob'd of her rest, and fool'd out of her fondness,
The Gentleman shall live, and if he love me,
Ye shall be both my triumphs; I will to him,
And as you carelessly fling off your fortune,
And now grow weary of my easie winning,
So will I lose the name of Valentine,
From henceforth all his flatteries, and believe it,

Since ye have so slightly parted with affection,
And that affection you have pawn'd your faith for;
From this hour no repentance, vows, nor prayers
Shall pluck me back again; what I shall do,
Yet I will undertake his cure, expect it,
Shall minister no comfort, no content
To either of ye, but hourly more vexations.

VALENTINE
Why, let him dye then.

CELLIDE
No, so much I have loved
To be commanded by you, that even now,
Even in my hate, I will obey your wishes.

VALENTINE
What shall I do?

CELLIDE
Dye like a fool unsorrow'd,
A bankrupt fool, that flings away his Treasure;
I must begin my cure.

VALENTINE
And I my Crosses.

[Exeunt.

ACTUS TERTIUS

SCÆNA PRIMA

Enter **FRANK**, sick, **PHYSICIANS** and an **APOTHECARY**.

1ST PHYSICIAN
Clap on the Cataplasm.

FRANK
Good Gentlemen,
Good learned Gentlemen.

2ND PHYSICIAN
And see these broths there,
Ready within this hour, pray keep your arms in,
The air is raw, and ministers much evil.

FRANCIS
'Pray leave me; I beseech ye leave me, Gentlemen,
I have no other sickness but your presence,
Convey your Cataplasms to those that need 'em,
Your Vomits, and your Clysters.

3RD PHYSICIAN
Pray be rul'd, Sir.

1ST PHYSICIAN
Bring in the Lettice Cap; you must be shaved, Sir,
And then how suddenly we'll make you sleep!

FRANK
Till dooms-day: what unnecessary nothings
Are these about a wounded mind?

2ND PHYSICIAN
How do ye?

FRANCIS
What questions they propound too! how do you, Sir?
I am glad to see you well.

3RD PHYSICIAN
A great distemper, it grows hotter still.

1ST PHYSICIAN
Open your mouth, I pray, Sir.

FRANK
And can you tell me
How old I am then? there's my hand, pray shew me
How many broken shins within this two year.
Who would be thus in fetters, good master Doctor,
And you dear Doctor, and the third sweet Doctor,
And precious master Apothecary, I do pray ye
To give me leave to live a little longer,
Ye stand before me like my Blacks.

2ND PHYSICIAN
'Tis dangerous,
For now his fancy turns too.

[Enter **CELLIDE**.

CELLIDE

By your leave Gentlemen:
And pray ye your leave a while too, I have something
Of secret to impart unto the Patient.

1ST PHYSICIAN
With all our hearts.

3RD PHYSICIAN
I mary such a Physick
May chance to find the humour: be not long Lady,
For we must minister within this half hour.

[Exit **PHYSICIANS**.

CELLIDE
You shall not stay for me.

FRANCIS
Would you were all rotten
That ye might only intend one anothers itches:
Or would the Gentlemen with one consent
Would drink small Beer but seven years, and abolish
That wild fire of the blood, unsatiate wenching,
That your two Indies, springs and falls might fail ye,
What torments these intruders into bodies.

CELLIDE
How do you worthy Sir?

FRANCIS
Bless me, what beams
Flew from these Angel eyes! O what a misery
What a most studied torment 'tis to me now
To be an honest man! dare ye sit by me?

CELLIDE
Yes, and do more than that too: comfort ye,
I see ye have need.

FRANCIS
You are a fair Physician:
You bring no bitterness gilt o're, to gull us,
No danger in your looks, yet there my death lyes.

CELLIDE
I would be sorry, Sir, my charity
And my good wishes for your health should merit
So stubborn a construction: will it please ye

To taste a little of this Cordial

[Enter **VALENTINE**.

For this I think must cure ye.

FRANCIS
Of which Lady?
Sure she has found my grief: why do you blush so?

CELLIDE
Do you not understand? of this, this Cordial.

VALENTINE
O my afflicted heart: she is gone for ever.

FRANCIS
What heaven have ye brought me Lady?

CELLIDE
Do not wonder:
For 'tis no impudence, nor want of honour
Makes me do this: but love to save your life, Sir,
Your life too excellent to lose in wishes,
Love, vertuous love.

FRANCIS
A vertuous blessing crown ye,
O goodly sweet, can there be so much charity
So noble a compassion in that heart
That's fill'd up with anothers fair affections?
Can mercy drop from those eyes?
Can miracles be wrought upon a dead man,
When all the power ye have, and perfect object
Lyes in anothers light, and his deserves it?

CELLIDE
Do not despair: nor do not think too boldly,
I dare abuse my promise, 'twas your friends
And so fast tyed, I thought no time could ruin:
But so much has your danger, and that spell
The powerful name of friend, prevail'd above him
To whom I ever owe obedience,
That here I am, by his command to cure ye,
Nay more for ever, by his full resignment,
And willingly I ratifie it.

FRANCIS

Hold for Heaven sake,
Must my friends misery make me a triumph?
Bear I that noble name, to be a Traitor?
O vertuous goodness, keep thy self untainted:
You have no power to yield, nor he to render,
Nor I to take: I am resolv'd to die first.

VALENTINE
Ha! saist thou so? nay then thou shalt not perish.

FRANCIS
And though I love ye above the light shines on me,
Beyond the wealth of Kingdoms, free content,
Sooner would snatch at such a blessing offer'd
Than at my pardon'd life by the law forfeited,
Yet, yet O noble Beauty, yet O Paradise
For you are all the wonder reveal'd of it,
Yet is a gratitude to be preserv'd,
A worthy gratitude to one most worthy
The name, and nobleness of friends.

CELLIDE
Pray tell me
If I had never known that Gentleman,
Would not you willingly embrace my offer?

FRANCIS
Do you make a doubt?

CELLIDE
And can ye be unwilling
He being old and impotent? his aim too
Levell'd at you, for your good? not constrain'd,
But out of cure, and counsel? Alas consider,
Play but the Woman with me, and consider
As he himself does, and I now dare see it,
Truly consider, Sir, what misery.

FRANCIS
For vertues sake take heed.

CELLIDE
What loss of youth,
What everlasting banishment from that
Our years do only covet to arrive at,
Equal affections and shot together:
What living name can dead age leave behind him,
What art of memory but fruitless doating?

FRANCIS
This cannot be.

CELLIDE
To you unless ye apply it
With more and firmer faith, and so digest it,
I speak but of things possible, not done
Nor like to be, a Posset cures your sickness,
And yet I know ye grieve this; and howsoever
The worthiness of friend may make ye stagger,
Which is a fair thing in ye, yet my Patient,
My gentle Patient, I would fain say more
If you would understand.

VALENTINE
O cruel Woman.

CELLIDE
Yet sure your sickness is not so forgetful,
Nor you so willing to be lost.

FRANCIS
Pray stay there:
Me thinks you are not fair now; me thinks more,
That modest vertue, men delivered of you,
Shews but like shadow to me, thin, and fading.

VALENTINE
Excellent friend.

FRANCIS
Ye have no share in goodness:
Ye are belyed; you are not Cellide,
The modest, immaculate: who are ye?
For I will know: what Devil, to do mischief
Unto my vertuous friend, hath shifted shapes
With that unblemished beauty?

CELLIDE
Do not rave, Sir,
Nor let the violence of thoughts distract ye,
You shall enjoy me: I am yours: I pity,
By those fair eyes I do.

FRANCIS
O double hearted!
O Woman, perfect Woman! what distraction

Was meant to mankind when thou was't made a Devil!
What an inviting Hell invented! tell me,
And if you yet remember what is goodness,
Tell me by that, and truth, can one so cherish'd
So sainted in the soul of him, whose service
Is almost turn'd to superstition,
Whose every day endeavours and desires
Offer themselves like Incense on your Altar,
Whose heart holds no intelligence, but holy
And most Religious with his love; whose life
(And let it ever be remembred Lady)
Is drawn out only for your ends.

VALENTINE
O miracle!

FRANCIS
Whose all, and every part of man: pray make me
Like ready Pages wait upon your pleasures;
Whose breath is but your bubble. Can ye, dare ye,
Must ye cast off this man, though he were willing,
Though in a nobleness, so cross my danger
His friendship durst confirm it, without baseness,
Without the stain of honour? shall not people
Say liberally hereafter, there's the Lady
That lost her Father, friend, herself, her faith too,
To fawn upon a stranger, for ought you know
As faithless as yourself, in love as fruitless.

VALENTINE
Take her with all my heart, thou art so honest
That 'tis most necessary I be undone.
With all my soul possess her.

[Exit **VALENTINE**.

CELLIDE
Till this minute,
I scorn'd, and hated ye, and came to cozen ye:
Utter'd those things might draw a wonder on me,
To make ye mad.

FRANCIS
Good Heaven, what is this Woman?

CELLIDE
Nor did your danger, but in charity,
Move me a whit: nor you appear unto me

More than a common object; yet now truly,
Truly, and nobly I do love ye dearly,
And from this hour ye are the man I honour,
You are the man, the excellence, the honesty,
The only friend, and I am glad your sickness
Fell so most happily at this time on ye,
To make this truth the worlds.

FRANCIS
Whither do you drive me?

CELLIDE
Back to your honesty, make that good ever,
'Tis like a strong built Castle, seated high,
That draws on all ambitions, still repair it,
Still fortifie it: there are thousand foes
Besides the Tyrant Beauty, will assail it:
Look to your Centinels that watch it hourly,
Your eyes, let them not wander.

FRANCIS
Is this serious?
Or does she play still with me?

CELLIDE
Keep your ears,
The two main Ports that may betray ye, strongly
From light belief first, then from flattery,
Especially where Woman beats the parley:
The body of your strength, your noble heart
From ever yielding to dishonest ends,
Rig'd round about with vertue, that no breaches,
No subtil mynes may meet ye.

FRANCIS
How like the Sun
Labouring in his Eclipse, dark, and prodigious,
She shew'd till now? when having won her way,
How full of wonder he breaks out again,
And sheds his vertuous beams: excellent Angel,
For no less can that heavenly mind proclaim thee,
Honour of all thy sex, let it be lawful,
And like a Pilgrim thus I kneel to beg it,
Not with prophane lips now, nor burnt affections,
But, reconcil'd to faith, with holy wishes,
To kiss that virgin hand.

CELLIDE

Take your desire, Sir,
And in a nobler way, for I dare trust ye,
No other fruit my love must ever yield ye,
I fear no more: yet your most constant memory
(So much I am wedded to that worthiness)
Shall ever be my Friend, Companion, Husband.
Farewel, and fairly govern your affections,
Stand, and deceive me not: O noble young man,
I love thee with my soul, but dare not say it:
Once more farewel, and prosper.

[Exit.

FRANCIS
Goodness guide thee:
My wonder like to fearful shapes in dreams,
Has wakened me out of my fit of folly,
But not to shake it off: a spell dwells in me,
A hidden charm shot from this beauteous Woman,
That fate can ne'r avoid, nor Physick find,
And by her counsel strengthen'd: only this
Is all the help I have, I love fair vertue.
Well, something I must do, to be a friend,
Yet I am poor, and tardy: something for her too
Though I can never reach her excellence,
Yet but to give an offer at a greatness.

[Enter **VALENTINE**, **THOMAS**, **HYLAS** and **SAM**.

VALENTINE
Be not uncivil Tom, and take your pleasure.

THOMAS
Do you think I am mad? you'l give me leave
To try her fairly?

VALENTINE
Do your best.

THOMAS
Why there Boy,
But where's the sick man?

HYLAS
Where are the Gentlewomen
That should attend him? there's the Patient.
Me thinks these Women—

THOMAS
Thou think'st nothing else.

VALENTINE
Go to him friend, and comfort him: I'le lead ye:
O my best joy, my worthiest friend, pray pardon me,
I am so over-joy'd I want expression:
I may live to be thankful: bid your friends welcome.

[Exit **VALENTINE**.

THOMAS
How do'st thou Frank? how do'st thou Boy? bear up man:
What, shrink i'th' sinews for a little sickness?
Deavolo morte.

FRANCIS
I am o'th' mending hand.

THOMAS
How like a Flute thou speak'st: o'th' mending hand man?
Gogs bores, I am well, speak like a man of worship.

FRANCIS
Thou art a mad companion: never staid Tom.

THOMAS
Let Rogues be staid that have no habitation,
A Gentleman may wander: sit thee down Frank,
And see what I have brought thee: come discover,
Open the Scene, and let the work appear.
A friend at need you Rogue is worth a million.

FRANCIS
What hast thou there, a julip?

HYLAS
He must not touch it,
'Tis present death.

THOMAS
Ye are an Ass, a twirepipe,
A Jeffery John bo peepe, thou mimister,
Thou mend a left-handed pack-saddle, out puppey,
My friend Frank, but a very foolish fellow:
Do'st thou see that Bottle? view it well.

FRANCIS

I do Tom.

THOMAS
There be as many lives in't, as a Cat carries,
'Tis everlasting liquor.

FRANCIS
What?

THOMAS
Old Sack, Boy,
Old reverend Sack, which for ought that I can read yet,
Was that Philosophers Stone the wise King Ptolomeus
Did all his wonders by.

FRANCIS
I see no harm Tom,
Drink with a moderation.

THOMAS
Drink with suger,
Which I have ready here, and here a glass boy,
Take me without my tools.

SAM
Pray Sir be temperate,
You know your own state best.

FRANCIS
Sir, I much thank ye,
And shall be careful: yet a glass or two
So fit I find my body, and that so needful.

THOMAS
Fill it, and leave your fooling: thou say'st true Frank.

HYLAS
Where are these Women I say?

THOMAS
'Tis most necessary,
Hang up your Julips and your Portugal Possets,
Your barley Broths, and sorrel Sops, they are mangy,
And breed the Scratches only: give me Sack:
I wonder where this Wench is though: have at thee.

HYLAS
So long, and yet no bolting?

FRANCIS
Do, I'le pledge thee.

THOMAS
Take it off thrice, and then cry heigh like a Huntsman
With a clear heart, and no more fits I warrant thee.
The only Cordial, Frank.

[**PHYSICIANS** and **SERVANT** within.

1ST PHYSICIAN
Are the things ready?
And is the Barber come?

SERVANT
An hour ago, Sir.

1ST PHYSICIAN
Bring out the Oyls then.

FRANCIS
Now or never Gentlemen,
Do me a kindness and deliver me.

THOMAS
From whom boy?

FRANCIS
From these things, that talk within there,
Physicians, Tom, Physicians, scowring-sticks,
They mean to read upon me.

[Enter three **PHYSICIANS**, **APOTHECARY** and **BARBER**.

HYLAS
Let 'em enter.

THOMAS
And be thou confident, we will deliver thee:
For look ye Doctor, say the Devil were sick now,
His horns saw'd off, and his head bound with a Biggin,
Sick of a Calenture, taken by a Surfeit
Of stinking souls at his Nephews, and St Dunstans,
What would you minister upon the sudden?
Your judgment short and sound.

1ST PHYSICIAN

A fools head.

THOMAS
No Sir,
It must be a Physicians for three causes,
The first because it is a bald-head likely,
Which will down easily without Applepap.

3RD PHYSICIAN
A main cause.

THOMAS
So it is, and well consider'd.
The second, for 'tis fill'd with broken Greek, Sir,
Which will so tumble in his stomach, Doctor,
And work upon the crudities, conceive me,
The fears, and the fiddle-strings within it,
That those damn'd souls must disembogue again.

HYLAS
Or meeting with the stygian humour.

THOMAS
Right, Sir.

HYLAS
Forc'd with a Cataplasm of Crackers.

THOMAS
Ever.

HYLAS
Scowre all before him, like a Scavenger.

THOMAS
Satis fecisti domine, my last cause,
My last is, and not least, most learned Doctors,
Because in most Physicians heads (I mean those
That are most excellent, and old withal,
And angry, though a Patient say his prayers,
And Paracelsians that do trade with poisons,
We have it by tradition of great writers)
There is a kind of Toad-stone bred, whose vertue
The Doctor being dri'd.

1ST PHYSICIAN
We are abus'd sirs.

HYLAS

I take it so, or shall be, for say the Belly-ake
Caus'd by an inundation of Pease-porridge,
Are we therefore to open the port Vein,
Or the port Esquiline?

SAM

A learned question:
Or grant the Diaphragma by a Rupture,
The sign being then in the head of Capricorn.

THOMAS

Meet with the passion Huperchondriaca,
And so cause a Carnosity in the Kidneyes.
Must not the brains, being butter'd with this humour—
Answer me that.

SAM

Most excellently argued.

2ND PHYSICIAN

The next fit you will have, my most fine Scholar,
Bedlam shall find a Salve for: fare ye well Sir,
We came to do you good, but these young Doctors
It seems have bor'd our Noses.

3RD PHYSICIAN

Drink hard Gentlemen,
And get unwholesome drabs: 'tis ten to one then
We shall hear further from ye, your note alter'd.

[Exeunt.

THOMAS

And wilt thou be gone, saies one?

HYLAS

And wilt thou be gone, saies t'other?

THOMAS

Then take the odd crown
To mend thy old Gown.

SAM

And we'l be gone all together.

FRANCIS

My learned Tom.

[Enter **SERVANT**.

SERVANT
Sir, the young Gentlewomen
Sent me to see what company ye had with ye,
They much desire to visit ye.

FRANCIS
Pray ye thank 'em,
And tell 'em my most sickness is their absence:
Ye see my company.

THOMAS
Come hither Crab,
What Gentlewomen are these? my Mistris?

SERVANT
Yes Sir.

HYLAS
And who else?

SERVANT
Mistress Alice.

HYLAS
Oh!

THOMAS
Hark ye sirrah,
No word of my being here, unless she know it.

SERVANT
I do not think she does.

THOMAS
Take that, and mum then.

SERVANT
You have ty'd my tongue up.

[Exit.

THOMAS
Sit you down good Francis,
And not a word of me till ye hear from me,
And as you find my humour, follow it:

You two come hither, and stand close, unseen Boys,
And do as I shall tutor ye.

FRANCIS
What, new work?

THOMAS
Prethee no more but help me now.

HYLAS
I would fain talk
With the Gentlewomen.

THOMAS
Talk with the Gentlewomen?
Of what forsooth? whose Maiden-head the last Mask
Suffer'd impression? or whose Clyster wrought best?
Take me as I shall tell thee.

HYLAS
To what end?
What other end came we along?

SAM
Be rul'd though.

THOMAS
Your weasel face must needs be ferretting
About the Farthing-ale;
Do as I bid ye,
Or by this light—

HYLAS
Come then.

THOMAS
Stand close and mark me.

FRANCIS
All this forc'd foolery will never do it.

[Enter **ALICE** and **MARY**.

ALICE
I hope we bring ye health, Sir: how is't with ye?

MARY
You look far better trust me, the fresh colour

Creeps now again into his cheeks.

ALICE
Your enemy
I see has done his worst. Come, we must have ye
Lusty again, and frolick man; leave thinking.

MARY
Indeed it does ye harm, Sir.

FRANCIS
My best visitants,
I shall be govern'd by ye.

ALICE
You shall be well then,
And suddenly, and soundly well.

MARY
This Air, Sir,
Having now season'd ye, will keep ye ever.

THOMAS
No, no, I have no hope, nor is it fit friends,
My life has been so lewd, my loose condition,
Which I repent too late, so lamentable,
That any thing but curses light upon me,
Exorbitant in all my wayes.

ALICE
Who's that, Sir,
Another sick man?

MARY
Sure I know that voice well.

THOMAS
In all my courses, careless disobedience.

FRANCIS
What a strange fellow's this?

THOMAS
No counsel friends,
No look before I leapt.

ALICE
Do you know the voyce, Sir?

FRANCIS
Yes, 'tis a Gentlemans that's much afflicted
In's mind: great pity Ladies.

ALICE
Now heaven help him.

FRANCIS
He came to me, to ask free pardon of me,
For some things done long since, which his distemper
Made to appear like wrong, but 'twas not so.

MARY
O that this could be truth.

HYLAS
Perswade your self.

THOMAS
To what end Gentlemen, when all is perish'd
Upon a wrack, is there a hope remaining?
The Sea, that ne'r knew sorrow, may be pitiful,
My credit's split, and sunk, nor is it possible,
Were my life lengthened out as long as—

MARY
I like this well.

SAM
Your mind is too mistrustful.

THOMAS
I have a vertuous Sister, but I scorn'd her,
A Mistris too, a noble Gentlewoman,
For goodness all out-going.

ALICE
Now I know him.

THOMAS
With these eyes friends, my eyes must never see more.

ALICE
This is for your sake Mary: take heed Cousin,
A man is not so soon made.

THOMAS

O my fortune!
But it is just, I be despis'd and hated.

HYLAS
Despair not, 'tis not manly: one hours goodness
Strikes off an infinite of ills.

ALICE
Weep truly
And with compassion, Cousin.

FRANCIS
How exactly
This cunning young Thief playes his part!

MARY
Well Tom,
My Tom again, if this be truth.

HYLAS
She weeps Boy.

THOMAS
O I shall die.

MARY
Now Heaven defend.

SAM
Thou hast her.

THOMAS
Come lead me to my Friend to take his farewel,
And then what fortune shall befal me, welcome,
How does it show?

HYLAS
O rarely well.

MARY
Say you so, Sir.

FRANCIS
O ye grand Ass.

MARY
And are ye there my Juggler?
Away we are abus'd, Alice.

ALICE
Fool be with thee.

[Exit **MARY** and **ALICE**.

THOMAS
Where is she?

FRANCIS
Gone; she found you out, and finely,
In your own noose she halter'd ye: you must be whispering
To know how things shew'd: not content to fare well
But you must roar out roast-meat; till that suspicion
You carried it most neatly, she believed too
And wept most tenderly; had you continu'd,
Without doubt you had brought her off.

THOMAS
This was thy Roguing,
For thou wert ever whispering: fye upon thee
Now could I break thy head.

HYLAS
You spoke to me first.

THOMAS
Do not anger me,
For by this hand I'le beat the buzard blind then.
She shall not scape me thus: farewel for this time.

FRANCIS
Good night, 'tis almost bed time: yet no sleep
Must enter these eyes, till I work a wonder.

[Exit.

THOMAS
Thou shalt along too, for I mean to plague thee
For this nights sins, I will never leave walking of thee
Till I have worn thee out.

HYLAS
Your will be done, Sir.

THOMAS
You will not leave me, Sam.

SAM
Not I.

THOMAS
Away then: I'le be your guide now, if my man be trusty,
My spightful Dame, I'le pipe ye such a huntsup
Shall make ye dance a tipvaes: keep close to me.

[Exeunt.

SCÆNA SECUNDA

Enter **SEBASTIAN** and **DOROTHEA**.

SEBASTIAN
Never perswade me, I will marry again,
What should I leave my state to, Pins and Poaking-sticks,
To Farthingals, and frownces? to fore-horses
And an old Leather Bawdy house behind 'em,
To thee?

DOROTHEA
You have a Son, Sir.

SEBASTIAN
Where, what is he?
Who is he like?

DOROTHEA
Your self.

SEBASTIAN
Thou lyest, thou hast marr'd him,
Thou, and thy prayer books: I do disclaim him:
Did not I take him singing yesternight
A godly Ballad, to a godly tune too,
And had a Catechism in's pocket, Damsel,
One of your dear disciples, I perceive it?
When did he ride abroad since he came over?
What Tavern has he us'd to? what things done
That shews a man, and mettle? when was my house
At such a shame before, to creep to bed
At ten a clock, and twelve, for want of company?
No singing, nor no dancing, nor no drinking?
Thou think'st not of these scandals; when, and where
Has he but shew'd his sword of late?

DOROTHEA
Despair not
I do beseech you, Sir, nor tempt your weakness,
For if you like it so, I can assure you
He is the same man still.

SEBASTIAN
Would thou wert ashes
On that condition; but believe it Gossip
You shall know you have wrong'd.

DOROTHEA
You never, Sir,
So well I know my duty: and for Heaven sake,
Take but this counsel with ye ere you marry,
You were wont to hear me: take him, and confess him,
Search him to the quick, and if you find him false,
Do as you please; a Mothers name I honour.

SEBASTIAN
He is lost, and spoil'd, I am resolv'd my roof
Shall never harbour him: and for you Minion
I'le keep you close enough, lest you break loose,
And do more mischief; get ye in: who waits?

[Exit **DOROTHEA**.

[Enter **SERVANT**.

SERVANT
Do you call, Sir?

SEBASTIAN
Seek the Boy: and bid him wait
My pleasure in the morning: mark what house
He is in, and what he does: and truly tell me.

SERVANT
I will not fail, Sir.

SEBASTIAN
If ye do, I'le hang ye.

[Exeunt.

Enter **THOMAS**, **HYLAS** and **SAM**.

THOMAS
Keep you the back door there, and be sure
None of her servants enter, or go out,
If any Woman pass, she is lawful prize, Boys,
Cut off all convoyes.

HYLAS
Who shall answer this?

THOMAS
Why, I shall answer it, you fearful widgeon,
I shall appear to th' action.

HYLAS
May we discourse too,
On honourable terms?

THOMAS
With any Gentlewoman
That shall appear at window: ye may rehearse too
By your commission safely, some sweet parcels
Of Poetry to a Chamber-maid.

HYLAS
May we sing too?
For there's my master-piece.

THOMAS
By no means, no Boys,
I am the man reserv'd for Air, 'tis my part,
And if she be not rock, my voyce shall reach her:
Ye may record a little, or ye may whistle,
As time shall minister, but for main singing,
Pray ye satisfie your selves: away, be careful.

HYLAS
But hark ye, one word Tom, we may be beaten.

THOMAS
That's as ye think good your selves: if you deserve it,
Why 'tis the easiest thing to compass: beaten?
What Bugbears dwell in thy brains? who should beat thee?

HYLAS

She has men enough.

THOMAS
Art not thou man enough too?
Thou hast flesh enough about thee: if all that mass
Will not maintain a little spirit, hang it,
And dry it too for dogs-meat: get you gone;
I have things of moment in my mind: that door,
Keep it as thou would'st keep thy Wife from a Servingman.
No more I say: away, Sam.

SAM
At your will, Sir.

[Exeunt **HYLAS** and **SAM**.

Enter **LAUNCELOT** and **FIDLER**.

LAUNCELOT
I have him here, a rare Rogue, good sweet Master,
Do something of some savour suddenly,
That we may eat, and live: I am almost starv'd,
No point manieur, no point devein, no Signieur,
Not by the vertue of my languages,
Nothing at my old masters to be hoped for,
O Signieur du, nothing to line my life with,
But cold Pyes with a cudgel, till you help us.

THOMAS
Nothing but famine frights thee: come hither Fidler,
What Ballads are you seen in best? be short Sir.

FIDLER
Under your masterships correction, I can sing
The Duke of Norfolk, or the merry Ballad
Of Diverus and Lazarus, the Rose of England,
In Creet when Dedimus first began,
Jonas his crying out against Coventry.

THOMAS
Excellent,
Rare matters all.

FIDLER
Mawdlin the Merchants Daughter,
The Devil, and ye dainty Dames.

THOMAS

Rare still.

FIDLER
The landing of the Spaniards at Bow,
With the bloudy battel at Mile-end.

THOMAS
All excellent:
No tuning as ye love me; let thy Fidle
Speak Welch, or any thing that's out of all tune,
The vilder still the better, like thy self,
For I presume thy voice will make no trees dance.

FIDLER
Nay truly, ye shall have it ev'n as homely.

THOMAS
Keep ye to that key, are they all abed trow?

LAUNCELOT
I hear no stirring any where, no light
In any window, 'tis a night for the nonce Sir.

THOMAS
Come strike up then: and say the Merchants daughter,
We'l bear the burthen: proceed to incision Fidler.

[Song.

[Enter **SERVANT**, above.

SERVANT
Who's there? what noise is this? what rogue
At these hours?

THOMAS
O what is that to you my fool?
O what is that to you,
Pluck in your face you bawling Ass,
Or I will break your brow.
Hey down, down, down.
A new Ballad, a new, a new.

FIDLER
The twelfth of April, on May day,
My house and goods were burnt away, &c.

[**MAID** above.

MAID
Why who is this?

LAUNCELOT
O damsel dear,
Open the door, and it shall appear,
Open the door.

MAID
O gentle squire.
I'le see thee hang'd first: farewel my dear,
'Tis master Thomas, there he stands.

[Enter **MARY** above.

MARY
'Tis strange
That nothing can redeem him: rail him hence,
Or sing him out in's own way, any thing
To be deliver'd of him.

MAID
Then have at him:
My man Thomas did me promise
He would visit me this night.

THOMAS
I am here Love, tell me dear Love,
How I may obtain thy sight.

MAID
Come up to my window love, come, come, come,
Come to my window my dear,
The wind, nor the rain shall trouble thee again,
But thou shalt be lodged here.

THOMAS
And art thou strong enough?

LAUNCELOT
Up, up, I warrant ye.

MARY
What do'st thou mean to do?

MAID
Good Mistress peace,

I'le warrant ye we'l cool him: Mary.

MARY (above)
I am ready.

THOMAS
The love of Greece, and it tickled him so,
That he devised a way to goe.
Now sing the Duke of Northumberland.

FIDLER
And climbing to promotion,
He fell down suddenly.

[**MARY** with a Devils vizard roaring, offers to kiss him, and he falls down.

MAID
Farewel Sir.

MARY
What hast thou done? thou hast broke his neck.

MAID
Not hurt him,
He pitcht upon his legs like a Cat.

THOMAS
O woman:
O miserable woman, I am spoil'd,
My leg, my leg, my leg, oh both my legs!

MARY
I told thee' what thou hadst done, mischief go with thee.

THOMAS
O I am lam'd for ever: O my leg,
Broken in twenty places: O take heed,
Take heed of women, Fidler: oh a Surgeon,
A Surgeon, or I dye: oh my good people,
No charitable people, all despightfull,
Oh what a misery am I in! oh my leg.

LAUNCELOT
Be patient Sir, be patient: let me bind it.

[Enter **SAM** and **HYLAS** with his head broken.

THOMAS

Oh do not touch it rogue.

HYLAS
My head, my head,
Oh my head's kill'd.

SAM
You must be courting wenches
Through key-holes, Captain Hylas, come and be comforted,
The skin is scarce broke.

THOMAS
O my leg.

SAM
How do ye Sir?

THOMAS
Oh maim'd for ever with a fall, he's spoil'd too,
I see his brains.

HYLAS
Away with me for Gods sake,
A Surgeon.

SAM
Here's a night indeed.

HYLAS
A Surgeon.

[Exit all but **FIDLER**.

[Enter **MARY** and **SERVANT** below.

MARY
Go run for help.

THOMAS
Oh.

MARY
Run all, and all too little,
O cursed beast that hurt him, run, run, flye,
He will be dead else.

THOMAS
Oh.

MARY
Good friend go you too.

FIDLER
Who pays me for my Musick?

MARY
Pox o' your Musick,
There's twelve pence for ye.

FIDLER
There's two groats again forsooth,
I never take above, and rest ye merry.

[Exit.

MARY
A grease pot guild your fidle strings: how do you,
How is my dear?

THOMAS
Why well I thank ye sweet heart,
Shall we walk in, for now there's none to trouble us?

MARY
Are ye so crafty, Sir? I shall meet with ye,
I knew your trick, and I was willing: my Tom,
Mine own Tom, now to satisfie thee, welcom, welcom,
Welcom my best friend to me, all my dearest.

THOMAS
Now ye are my noble Mistress: we lose time sweet.

MARY
I think they are all gone.

THOMAS
All, ye did wisely.

MARY
And you as craftily.

THOMAS
We are well met Mistress.

MARY
Come, let's goe in then lovingly: O my Skarf Tom.

I lost it thereabout, find it, and wear it
As your poor Mistress favour.

[Exit.

THOMAS
I am made now,
I see no venture is in no hand: I have it,
How now? the door lock't, and she in before?
Am I so trim'd?

MARY
One parting word sweet Thomas,
Though to save your credit, I discharg'd your Fidler,
I must not satisfie your folly too Sir,
Ye'are subtle, but believe it Fox, I'le find ye,
The Surgeons will be here straight, roar again boy,
And break thy legs for shame, thou wilt be sport else,
Good night.

THOMAS
She saies most true, I must not stay: she has bob'd me,
Which if I live, I'le recompence, and shortly,
Now for a Ballad to bring me off again.
All young men be warn'd by me, how you do goe a wooing.
Seek not to climb, for fear ye fall, thereby comes your undoing, &c.

[Exeunt.

ACTUS QUARTUS

SCÆNA PRIMA

Enter **VALENTINE**, **ALICE** and **SERVANT**.

VALENTINE
He cannot goe and take no farewel of me,
Can he be so unkind? he's but retir'd
Into the Garden or the Orchard: see Sirs.

ALICE
He would not ride there certain, those were planted
Only for walks I take it.

VALENTINE
Ride? nay then,

Had he a horse out?

SERVANT
So the Groom delivers
Somewhat before the break of day.

VALENTINE
He's gone,
My best friend's gone Alice; I have lost the noblest,
The truest, and the most man I e're found yet.

ALICE
Indeed Sir, he deserves all praise.

VALENTINE
All Sister,
All, all, and all too little: O that honesty,
That ermine honesty, unspotted ever,
That perfect goodness.

ALICE
Sure he will return Sir,
He cannot be so harsh.

VALENTINE
O never, never,
Never return, thou know'st not where the cause lyes.

ALICE
He was the worthiest welcom.

VALENTINE
He deserv'd it.

ALICE
Nor wanted, to our knowledge.

VALENTINE
I will tell thee,
Within this hour, things that shall startle thee,
He never must return.

[Enter **MICHAEL**.

MICHAEL
Good morrow Signieur.

VALENTINE

Good morrow Master Michael.

MICHAEL
My good neighbour,
Me thinks you are stirring early since your travel,
You have learn'd the rule of health sir, where's your mistress?
She keeps her warm I warrant ye, i' bed yet?

VALENTINE
I think she does.

ALICE
'Tis not her hour of waking.

MICHAEL
Did you lye with her, Lady?

ALICE
Not to night Sir,
Nor any night this week else.

MICHAEL
When last saw ye her?

ALICE
Late yesternight.

MICHAEL
Was she 'bed then?

ALICE
No Sir,
I left her at her prayers: why do ye ask me?

MICHAEL
I have been strangely haunted with a dream
All this long night, and after many wakings,
The same dream still; me thought I met young Cellide
Just at S. Katherines gate the Nunnery.

VALENTINE
Ha?

MICHAEL
Her face slubber'd o're with tears, and troubles,
Me thought she cry'd unto the Lady Abbess,
For charity receive me holy woman,
A Maid that has forgot the worlds affections,

Into thy virgin order: me thought she took her,
Put on a Stole, and sacred robe upon her,
And there I left her.

VALENTINE
Dream?

MICHAEL
Good Mistress Alice
Do me the favour (yet to satisfie me)
To step but up, and see.

ALICE
I know she's there Sir,
And all this but a dream.

MICHAEL
You know not my dreams,
They are unhappy ones, and often truths,
But this I hope, yet.

ALICE
I will satisfie ye.

[Exit.

MICHAEL
Neighbours, how does the Gentleman?

VALENTINE
I know not,
Dream of a Nunnery?

MICHAEL
How found ye my words
About the nature of his sickness Valentine?

VALENTINE
Did she not cry out, 'twas my folly too
That forc'd her to this nunnery? did she not curse me?
For God sake speak: did you not dream of me too,
How basely, poorly, tamely, like a fool,
Tir'd with his joyes?

MICHAEL
Alas poor Gentleman,
Ye promis'd me Sir to bear all these crosses.

VALENTINE
I bear 'em till I break again.

MICHAEL
But nobly,
Truly to weigh.

VALENTINE
Good neighbours, no more of it,
Ye do but fling flax on my fire: where is she?

[Enter **ALICE**.

ALICE
Not yonder Sir, nor has not this night certain
Been in her bed.

MICHAEL
It must be truth she tells ye,
And now I'le shew ye why I came: this morning
A man of mine being employed about business,
Came early home, who at S. Katherines Nunnery,
About day peep, told me he met your Mistress,
And as I spoke it in a dream, so troubled
And so received by the Abbess, did he see her,
The wonder made me rise, and hast unto ye
To know the cause.

VALENTINE
Farewel, I cannot speak it.

[Exit **VALENTINE**.

ALICE
For Heaven sake leave him not.

MICHAEL
I will not Lady.

ALICE
Alas, he's much afflicted.

MICHAEL
We shall know shortly more, apply your own care
At home good Alice, and trust him to my counsel,
Nay, do not weep, all shall be well, despair not.

[Exeunt.

SCÆNA SECUNDA

Enter **SEBASTIAN** and a **SERVANT**.

SEBASTIAN
At Valentines house so merry?

SERVANT
As a pie Sir.

SEBASTIAN
So gamesom dost thou say?

SERVANT
I am sure I heard it.

SEBASTIAN
Ballads, and Fidles too?

SERVANT
No, but one Fidle;
But twenty noyses.

[Enter **LAUNCELOT**.

SEBASTIAN
Did he do devises?

SERVANT
The best devises Sir: here's my fellow Launcelot
He can inform ye all: he was among 'em,
A mad thing too: I stood but in a corner.

SEBASTIAN
Come Sir, what can you say? is there any hope yet
Your Master may return?

LAUNCELOT
He went far else,
I will assure your worship on my credit
By the faith of a Travellor, and a Gentleman,
Your son is found again, the son, the Tom.

SEBASTIAN
Is he the old Tom?

LAUNCELOT
The old Tom.

SEBASTIAN
Go forward.

LAUNCELOT
Next, to consider how he is the old Tom.

SEBASTIAN
Handle me that.

LAUNCELOT
I would ye had seen it handled
Last night Sir, as we handled it: cap à pe,
Footra for leers, and learings; O the noise,
The noise we made.

SEBASTIAN
Good, good.

LAUNCELOT
The windows clattering
And all the Chambermaids in such a whobub,
One with her smock half off, another in hast
With a serving-mans hose upon her head.

SEBASTIAN
Good still.

LAUNCELOT
A fellow railing out of a loop-hole there,
And his mouth stopt with durt.

SEBASTIAN
I' faith a fine Boy.

LAUNCELOT
Here one of our heads broke.

SEBASTIAN
Excellent good still.

LAUNCELOT
The Gentleman himself, young M. Thomas,
Inviron'd with his furious Myrmidons
The fiery Fidler, and my self; now singing,

Now beating at the door, there parlying,
Courting at that window, at the other scalling
And all these several noises to two Trenchers,
Strung with a bottom of brown thred, which show'd admirable.

SEBASTIAN
There eat, and grow again, I am pleas'd.

LAUNCELOT
Nor here Sir,
Gave we the frolick over: though at length
We quit the Ladies Skonce on composition;
But to the silent streets we turn'd our furies:
A sleeping watchman here we stole the shooes from,
There made a noise, at which he wakes, and follows:
The streets are durty, takes a queen-hith cold,
Hard cheese, and that choaks him o' Munday next:
Windows, and signs we sent to Erebus;
A crue of bawling curs we entertain'd last,
When having let the pigs loose in out parishes,
O the brave cry we made as high as Algate!
Down comes a Constable, and the Sow his Sister
Most traiterously tramples upon Authority,
There a whole stand of rug gowns rowted manly
And the Kings peace put to flight: a purblind pig here
Runs me his head into the Admirable Lanthorn,
Out goes the light, and all turns to confusion:
A potter rises, to enquire this passion,
A Boar imbost takes sanctuary in his shop,
When twenty dogs rush after, we still cheering,
Down goe the pots, and pipkins, down the pudding pans,
The cream-bolls cry revenge here, there the candlesticks.

SEBASTIAN
If this be true, thou little tyney page,
This tale that thou tell'st me,
Then on thy back will I presently hang
A handsom new Livery:
But if this be false, thou little tyney page
As false it well may be,
Then with a cudgel of four foot long
I'le beat thee from head to toe.

[Enter **SERVANT**.

SEBASTIAN
Will the boy come?

SERVANT
He will Sir.

[Enter **THOMAS**.

SEBASTIAN
Time tries all then.

LAUNCELOT
Here he comes now himself Sir.

SEBASTIAN
To be short Thomas,
Because I feel a scruple in my conscience
Concerning thy demeanour, and a main one,
And therefore like a Father would be satisfi'd,
Get up to that window there, and presently
Like a most compleat Gentleman, come from Tripoly.

THOMAS
Good Lord Sir, how are you misled: what fancies
(Fitter for idle boys, and drunkards, let me speak't,
And with a little wonder I beseech you)
Choak up your noble judgement?

SEBASTIAN
You Rogue Launcelot,
You lying Rascal.

LAUNCELOT
Will ye spoil all again Sir.
Why, what a Devil do you mean?

THOMAS
Away knave,
Ye keep a company of sawcy fellows,
Debosh'd, and daily drunkards, to devour ye,
Things, whose dull souls, tend to the Celler only,
Ye are ill advis'd Sir, to commit your credit.

SEBASTIAN
Sirrah, Sirrah.

LAUNCELOT
Let me never eat again Sir,
Nor feel the blessing of another blew-coat,
If this young Gentleman, sweet Master Thomas,
Be not as mad as heart can wish: your heart Sir,

If yesternights discourse: speak fellow Robin,
And if thou speakest less than truth.

THOMAS
'Tis strange these varlets.

SERVANT
By these ten bones Sir, if these eyes, and ears
Can hear and see.

THOMAS
Extream strange, should thus boldly
Bud in your sight, unto your son.

LAUNCELOT
O deu guin
Can ye deny, ye beat a Constable
Last night?

THOMAS
I touch Authoritie, ye Rascal?
I violate the Law?

LAUNCELOT
Good Master Thomas.

SERVANT
Did you not take two wenches from the watch too
And put 'em into pudding lane?

LAUNCELOT
We mean not
Those civil things you did at M. Valentines,
The Fiddle, and the fa'las.

THOMAS
O strange impudence!
I do beseech you Sir give no such licence
To knaves and drunkards, to abuse your son thus:
Be wise in time, and turn 'em off: we live Sir
In a State govern'd civilly, and soberly,
Where each mans actions should confirm the Law,
Not crack, and cancel it.

SEBASTIAN
Lancelot du Lake,
Get you upon adventures: cast your coat
And make your exit.

LAUNCELOT
Pur lamour de dieu.

SEBASTIAN
Pur me no purs: but pur at that door, out Sirrah,
I'le beat ye purblind else, out ye eight languages.

LAUNCELOT
My bloud upon your head.

[Exit **LAUNCELOT**.

THOMAS
Purge me 'em all Sir.

SEBASTIAN
And you too presently.

THOMAS
Even as you please Sir.

SEBASTIAN
Bid my maid servant come, and bring my Daughter,
I will have one shall please me.

[Exit **SERVANT**.

THOMAS
'Tis most fit Sir.

SEBASTIAN
Bring me the mony there: here M. Thomas.

[Enter two **SERVANTS** with two bags.

I pray sit down, ye are no more my son now,
Good Gentleman be cover'd.

THOMAS
At your pleasure.

SEBASTIAN
This mony I do give ye, because of whilom
You have been thought my son, and by my self too,
And some things done like me: ye are now another:
There is two hundred pound, a civil summe
For a young civil man: much land and Lordship

Will as I take it now, but prove temptation
To dread ye from your setled, and sweet carriage.

THOMAS
You say right Sir.

SEBASTIAN
Nay I beseech ye cover.

THOMAS
At your dispose: and I beseech ye too Sir,
For the word civil, and more setled course
It may but put to use, that on the interest
Like a poor Gentleman.

SEBASTIAN
It shall, to my use,
To mine again: do you see Sir: good fine Gentleman,
I give no brooding mony for a Scrivener,
Mine is for present traffick, and so I'le use it.

THOMAS
So much for that then.

[Enter **DOROTHEA** and four **MAIDS**.

SEBASTIAN
For the main cause Monsieur,
I sent to treat with you about, behold it;
Behold that piece of story work, and view it.
I want a right heir to inherit me,
Not my estate alone, but my conditions,
From which you are revolted, therefore dead,
And I will break my back, but I will get one.

THOMAS
Will you choose there Sir?

SEBASTIAN
There, among those Damsels,
In mine own tribe: I know their qualities
Which cannot fail to please me: for their beauties
A matter of a three farthings, makes all perfect,
A little beer, and beef broth: they are sound too.
Stand all a breast: now gentle M. Thomas
Before I choose, you having liv'd long with me,
And happily sometimes with some of these too,
Which fault I never frown'd upon; pray shew me

(For fear we confound our Genealogies)
Which have you laid aboord? speak your mind freely,
Have you had copulation with that Damsel?

THOMAS
I have.

SEBASTIAN
Stand you aside then: how with her Sir?

THOMAS
How, is not seemly here to say.

DOROTHEA
Here's fine sport.

SEBASTIAN
Retire you too: speak forward M. Thomas.

THOMAS
I will: and to the purpose; even with all Sir.

SEBASTIAN
With all? that's somewhat large.

DOROTHEA
And yet you like it.
Was ever sin so glorious?

SEBASTIAN
With all Thomas?

THOMAS
All surely Sir.

SEBASTIAN
A sign thou art mine own yet,
In again all: and to your several functions.

[Exit **MAIDS**.

What say you to young Luce, my neighbours Daughter,
She was too young I take it, when you travel'd;
Some twelve years old?

THOMAS
Her will was fifteen Sir.

SEBASTIAN
A pretty answer, to cut off long discourse,
For I have many yet to ask ye of,
Where I can choose, and nobly, hold up your finger
When ye are right: what say ye to Valeria
Whose husband lies a dying now? why two,
And in that form?

THOMAS
Her husband is recover'd.

SEBASTIAN
A witty moral: have at ye once more Thomas,
The Sisters of St. Albons, all five; dat boy,
Dat's mine own boy.

DOROTHEA
Now out upon thee Monster.

THOMAS
Still hoping of your pardon.

SEBASTIAN
There needs none man:
A straw on pardon: prethee need no pardon:
I'le aske no more, nor think no more of marriage,
For o' my conscience I shall be thy Cuckold:
There's some good yet left in him: bear your self well,
You may recover me, there's twenty pound Sir,
I see some sparkles which may flame again,
You may eat with me when you please, you know me.

[Exit **SEBASTIAN**.

DOROTHEA
Why do you lye so damnably, so foolishly?

THOMAS
Do'st thou long to have thy head broke? hold thy peace
And do as I would have thee, or by this hand
I'le kill thy Parrat, hang up thy small hand,
And drink away thy dowry to a penny.

DOROTHEA
Was ever such a wilde Asse?

THOMAS
Prethee be quiet.

DOROTHEA
And do'st thou think men will not beat thee monstrously
For abusing their wives and children?

THOMAS
And do'st thou think
Mens wives and children can be abus'd too much?

DOROTHEA
I wonder at thee.

THOMAS
Nay, thou shalt adjure me
Before I have done.

DOROTHEA
How stand ye with your mistress?

THOMAS
I shall stand nearer
E're I be twelve hours older: there's my business,
She is monstrous subtile Dol.

DOROTHEA
The Devil I think
Cannot out-subtile thee.

THOMAS
If he play fair play,
Come, you must help me presently.

DOROTHEA
I discard ye.

THOMAS
Thou shalt not sleep nor eat.

DOROTHEA
I'le no hand with ye,
No bawd to your abuses.

THOMAS
By this light Dol,
Nothing but in the way of honesty.

DOROTHEA
Thou never knew'st that road: I hear your vigils.

THOMAS
Sweet honey Dol, if I do not marry her,
Honestly marry her, if I mean not honourably,
Come, thou shalt help me, take heed how you vex me,
I'le help thee to a husband too, a fine Gentleman,
I know thou art mad, a tall young man, a brown man,
I swear he has his maidenhead, a rich man.

DOROTHEA
You may come in to dinner, and I'le answer ye.

THOMAS
Nay I'le go with thee Dol: four hundred a year wench.

[Exeunt.

SCÆNA TERTIA

Enter **MICHAEL** and **VALENTINE**.

MICHAEL
Good Sir go back again, and take my counsel,
Sores are not cur'd by sorrows, nor time broke from us,
Pull'd back again by sighs.

VALENTINE
What should I do friend?

MICHAEL
Do that that may redeem ye, go back quickly,
Sebastians Daughter can prevail much with her,
The Abbess is her Aunt too.

VALENTINE
But my friend then
Whose love and loss is equal ty'd.

MICHAEL
Content ye,
That shall be my task if he be alive,
Or where my travel and my care may reach him,
I'le bring him back again.

VALENTINE
Say he come back

To piece his poor friends life out? and my Mistress
Be vow'd for ever a recluse?

MICHAEL
So suddenly
She cannot, hast ye therefore instantly away Sir,
To put that Daughter by; first as to a Father,
Then as a friend she was committed to ye,
And all the care she now has: by which priviledge
She cannot do her this violence,
But you may break it, and the law allows ye.

VALENTINE
O but I forc'd her to it.

MICHAEL
Leave disputing
Against your self, if you will needs be miserable
Spight of her goodness, and your friends perswasions.
Think on, and thrive thereafter.

VALENTINE
I will home then.
And follow your advice, and good, good Michael.

MICHAEL
No more, I know your soul's divided, Valentine,
Cure but that part at home with speedy marriage
E're my return, for then those thoughts that vext her,
While there ran any stream for loose affections,
Will be stopt up, and chaste ey'd honour guide her.
Away, and hope the best still: I'le work for ye,
And pray too heartily, away, no more words.

[Exeunt.

SCÆNA QUARTA

Enter **HYLAS** and **SAM**.

HYLAS
I care not for my broken head,
But that it should be his plot, and a wench too,
A lowzie, lazie wench prepar'd to do it.

SAM

Thou hadst as good be quiet, for o' my conscience
He'l put another on thee else.

HYLAS
I am resolv'd
To call him to account, was it not manifest
He meant a mischief to me, and laughed at me,
When he lay roaring out, his leg was broken,
And no such matter? had he broke his neck,
Indeed 'twould ne'r have griev'd me; gallows gall him.
Why should he chuse out me?

SAM
Thou art ever ready
To thrust thy self into these she occasions,
And he as full of knavery to accept it.

HYLAS
Well, if I live I'll have a new trick for him.

SAM
That will not be amiss, but to fight with him
Is to no purpose; besides, he's truly valiant,
And a most deadly hand; thou never fought'st yet,
Nor o' my Conscience hast no faith in fighting.

HYLAS
No, no, I will not fight.

SAM
Besides the quarrel,
Which has a woman in't to make it scurvy,
Who would lye stinking in a Surgeons hands,
A month or two this weather? for believe it,
He never hurts under a quarters healing.

HYLAS
No, upon better thought, I will not fight, Sam,
But watch my time.

SAM
To pay him with a project;
Watch him too, I would wish ye; prithee tell me,
Dost thou affect these women still?

HYLAS
Yes, 'faith, Sam,
I love 'em ev'n as well as e'r I did,

Nay, if my brains were beaten out, I must to 'em.

SAM
Dost thou love any woman?

HYLAS
Any woman
Of what degree or calling.

SAM
Of any age too?

HYLAS
Of any age, from fourscore to fourteen, Boy,
Of any fashion.

SAM
And defect too?

HYLAS
Right,
For those I love to lead me to repentance;
A woman with no Nose, after my surquedry,
Shews like King Philip's Moral, Memento mori;
And she that has a wooden leg, demonstrates
Like Hypocrites, we halt before the gallows;
An old one with one tooth, seems to say to us,
Sweets meats have sowr sauce; she that's full of aches,
Crum not your Bread before you taste your Porridge,
And many morals we may find.

SAM
'Tis well, Sir,
Ye make so worthy uses; but quid igitur,
What shall we now determine?

HYLAS
Let's consider
An hour or two how I may fit this fellow.

SAM
Let's find him first, he'll quickly give occasion,
But take heed to your self, and say I warn'd ye;
He has a plaguey pate.

HYLAS
That at my danger.

[Exeunt.

[Musick.

Enter **SAYLERS** singing, to them **MICHAEL** and **FRANCIS**.

SAYLERS
Aboard, aboard, the wind stands fair.

MICHAEL
These call for Passengers, I'll stay and see
What men they take aboard.

FRANCIS
A Boat, a Boat, a Boat.

SAYLERS
Away then.

FRANCIS
Whither are ye bound, Friends?

SAYLERS
Down to the Straits.

MICHAEL
Ha! 'tis not much unlike him.

FRANCIS
May I have passage for my money?

SAYLERS
And welcome too.

MICHAEL
'Tis he, I know 'tis he now.

FRANCIS
Then merrily aboard, and noble friend,
Heavens goodness keep thee ever, and all vertue
Dwell in thy bosome, Cellide, my last tears
I leave behind me thus, a sacrifice,
For I dare stay no longer to betray ye.

MICHAEL
Be not so quick, Sir; Saylers I here charge ye
By virtue of this Warrant, as you will answer it,
For both your Ship and Merchant I know perfectly,
Lay hold upon this fellow.

FRANCIS
Fellow?

MICHAEL
I, Sir.

SAYLERS
No hand to Sword, Sir, we shall master ye,
Fetch out the manacles.

FRANCIS
I do obey ye;
But I beseech you, Sir, inform me truly
How I am guilty.

MICHAEL
You have rob'd a Gentleman,
One that you are bound to for your life and being;
Money and horse unjustly ye took from him,
And something of more note, but—for y'are a Gentleman.

FRANCIS
It shall be so, and here I'll end all miseries,
Since friendship is so cruel, I confess it,
And which is more, a hundred of these robberies:
This Ring I stole too from him, and this Jewel,
The first and last of all my wealth; forgive me
My innocence and truth, for saying I stole 'em,
And may they prove of value but to recompence
The thousandth part of his love, and bread I have eaten;
'Pray see 'em render'd noble Sir, and so
I yield me to your power.

MICHAEL
Guard him to th' water,
I charge you, Saylers, there I will receive him,
And back convey him to a Justice.

SAYLERS
Come, Sir,
Look to your neck, you are like to sail i'th' air now.

[Exeunt.

SCÆNA SEXTA

Enter **THOMAS**, **DOROTHEA** and **MAID**.

THOMAS
Come quickly, quickly, paint me handsomely,
Take heed my nose be not in grain too;
Come Doll, Doll, disen me.

DOROTHEA
If you should play now
Your Devils parts again.

THOMAS
Yea and nay, Dorothea.

DOROTHEA
If ye do any thing, but that ye have sworn to,
Which only is access.

THOMAS
As I am a Gentleman;
Out with this hair, Doll, handsomely.

DOROTHEA
You have your Breeches?

THOMAS
I prithee away, thou know'st I am monstrous ticklish,
What, dost thou think I love to blast my Buttocks?

DOROTHEA
I'll plague ye for this Roguery; for I know well
What ye intend, Sir.

THOMAS
On with my muffler.

DOROTHEA
Ye are a sweet Lady; come, let's see you courtesie;
What, broke i'th bum? hold up your head.

THOMAS
Plague on't,

I shall bepiss my Breeches if I cowr thus,
Come, I am ready.

MAID
At all points as like, Sir,
As if you were my Mistress.

DOROTHEA
Who goes with ye?

THOMAS
None but my fortune, and my self.

[Exit **THOMAS**.

DOROTHEA
'Bless ye:
Now run for thy life, and get before him,
Take the by-way, and tell my Cousin Mary
In what shape he intends to come to cozen her;
I'll follow at thy heels my self, fly Wench.

MAID
I'll do it.

[Exit.

[Enter **SEBASTIAN** and **THOMAS**.

DOROTHEA
My Father has met him; this goes excellent,
And I'll away in time; look to your Skin, Thomas.

[Exit.

SEBASTIAN
What, are you grown so corn fed, Goody Gillian,
You will not know your Father? what vagaries
Have you in hand? what out-leaps, durty heels,
That at these hours of night ye must be gadding,
And through the Orchard take your private passage?
What, is the breeze in your Breech? or has your Brother
Appointed you an hour of meditation
How to demean himself; get ye to bed, drab,
Or I'll so crab your Shoulders; ye demure Slut,
Ye civil dish of sliced Beef, get ye in.

THOMAS

I wi' not, that I wi' not.

SEBASTIAN
Is't ev'n so, Dame?
Have at ye with a night Spell then.

THOMAS
'Pray hold, Sir.

SEBASTIAN
St. George, St. George, our Ladies Knight,
He walks by day, so does he by night,
And when he had her found,
He her beat, and her bound,
Until to him her troth she plight,
She would not stir from him that night.

THOMAS
Then have at ye with a Counter Spell,
From Elves, Hobs, and Fayries, that trouble our Dayries,
From Fire-Drakes and Fiends, and such as the Devil sends,
Defend us good Heaven.

[Exit.

[Enter **LAUNCELOT**.

LAUNCELOT
Bless me master; look up, Sir, I beseech ye,
Up with your eyes to heaven.

SEBASTIAN
Up with your nose, Sir,
I do not bleed, 'twas a sound knock she gave me,
A plaguey mankind Girl, how my brain totters?
Well, go thy ways, thou hast got one thousand pound more
With this dog trick,
Mine own true spirit in her too.

LAUNCELOT
In her? alas Sir,
Alas poor Gentlewoman, she a hand so heavy,
To knock ye like a Calf down, or so brave a courage
To beat her father? if you could believe, Sir.

SEBASTIAN
Who would'st thou make me believe it was, the Devil?

LAUNCELOT
One that spits fire as fast as he sometimes, Sir,
And changes shapes as often; your Son Thomas;
Never wonder, if it be not he, straight hang me.

SEBASTIAN
He? if it be so,
I'll put thee in my Will, and there's an end on't.

LAUNCELOT
I saw his legs, h'as Boots on like a Player,
Under his wenches cloaths, 'tis he, 'tis Thomas
In his own Sisters Cloaths, Sir, and I can wast him.

SEBASTIAN
No more words then, we'll watch him, thou'lt not believe
Launce,
How heartily glad I am.

LAUNCELOT
May ye be gladder,
But not this way, Sir.

SEBASTIAN
No more words, but watch him.

[Exeunt.

SCÆNA SEPTIMA

Enter **MARY**, **DOROTHEA** and **MAID**.

MARY
When comes he?

DOROTHEA
Presently.

MARY
Then get you up, Doll,
Away, I'll straight come to you: is all ready?

MAID
All.

MARY

Let the light stand far enough.

MAID
'Tis placed so.

MARY
Stay you to entertain him to his chamber,
But keep close, Wench, he flyes at all.

MAID
I warrant ye.

MARY
You need no more instruction?

MAID
I am perfect.

[Exeunt.

SCÆNA OCTAVIA

Enter **VALENTINE** and **THOMAS**.

THOMAS
More stops yet? sure the fiend's my ghostly father,
Old Valentine; what wind's in his poop?

VALENTINE
Lady,
You are met most happily; O gentle Doll,
You must now do me an especial favour.

THOMAS
What is it master Valentine? I am sorely troubled
With a salt rheum faln i' my gums.

VALENTINE
I'll tell ye,
And let it move you equally; my blest Mistress,
Upon a slight occasion taking anger,
Took also (to undo me) your Aunts Nunnery,
From whence by my perswasion to redeem her,
Will be impossible: nor have I liberty
To come and visit her; my good, good Dorothea,
You are most powerful with her, and your Aunt too,

And have access at all hours liberally,
Speak now or never for me.

THOMAS
In a Nunnery?
That course must not be suffered, Master Valentine,
Her Mother never knew it; rare sport for me;
Sport upon sport, by th' break of day I'll meet ye,
And fear not, Man, we'll have her out I warrant ye,
I cannot stay now.

VALENTINE
You will not break?

THOMAS
By no means.
Good night.

VALENTINE
Good night kind Mistress Doll.

[Exit.

THOMAS
This thrives well,
Every one takes me for my Sister, excellent;
This Nunnery's faln so pat too, to my figure,
Where there be handsome wenches, and they shall know it,
If once I creep in, ere they get me out again;
Stay, here's the house, and one of her Maids.

[Enter **MAID**.

MAID
Who's there?
O Mistress Dorothea! you are a stranger.

THOMAS
Still Mistress Dorothea? this geer will cotton.

MAID
Will you walk in, Forsooth?

THOMAS
Where is your Mistress?

MAID
Not very well; she's gone to bed, I am glad

You are come so fit to comfort her.

THOMAS
Yes, I'll comfort her.

MAID
'Pray make not much noise, for she is sure asleep,
You know your side, creep softly in, your company
Will warm her well.

THOMAS
I warrant thee I'll warm her.

MAID
Your Brother has been here, the strangest fellow.

THOMAS
A very Rogue, a rank Rogue.

MAID
I'll conduct ye
Even to her Chamber-door, and there commit ye.

[Exeunt.

SCÆNA NONUS

Enter **MICHAEL**, **FRANCIS** and **OFFICERS**.

MICHAEL
Come Sir, for this night I shall entertain ye,
And like a Gentleman, how e'r your fortune
Hath cast ye on the worst part.

FRANCIS
How you please, Sir,
I am resolv'd, nor can a joy or misery
Much move me now.

MICHAEL
I am angry with my self now
For putting this forc'd way upon his patience,
Yet any other course had been too slender:
Yet what to think I know not, for most liberally
He hath confess'd strange wrongs, which if they prove so,
How e'r the others long love may forget all,

Yet 'twas most fit he should come back, and this way.
Drink that; and now to my care leave your Prisoner,
I'll be his guard for this night.

OFFICERS
Good night to your Worship.

MICHAEL
Good night, my honest friends; come, Sir, I hope
There shall be no such cause of such a sadness
As you put on.

FRANCIS
'Faith, Sir, my rest is up,
And what I now pull shall no more afflict me
Than if I plaid at span-Counter, nor is my face
The map of any thing I seem to suffer,
Lighter affections seldom dwell in me, Sir.

MICHAEL
A constant Gentleman; would I had taken
A Feaver when I took this harsh way to disturb him.
Come, walk with me, Sir, ere to morrow night
I doubt not but to see all this blown over.

[Exeunt.

ACTUS QUINTUS

SCÆNA PRIMA

Enter **HYLAS**.

HYLAS
I have dog'd his Sister, sure 'twas she,
And I hope she will come back again this night too;
Sam I have lost of purpose; now if I can
With all the art I have, as she comes back,
But win a parley for my broken Pate,
Off goes her maiden-head, and there's vindicta.
They stir about the house, I'll stand at distance.

[Exit.

[Enter **MARY** and **DOROTHEA**, and then **THOMAS** and **MAID**.

DOROTHEA
Is he come in?

MARY
Speak softly,
He is, and there he goes.

THOMAS
Good night, good night, Wench.

[A Bed discovered with a Black-**MOOR** in it.

MAID
As softly as you can.

[Exit.

THOMAS
I'll play the mouse, Nan,
How close the little thief lies!

MARY
How he itches!

DOROTHEA
What would you give now to be there, and I
At home, Mall?

MARY
Peace for shame.

THOMAS
In what a figure
The little fool has pull'd it self together!
Anon you will lye straighter;
Ha! there's rare circumstance
Belongs to such a treatise; do ye tumble?
I'll tumble with ye straight, wench: she sleeps soundly,
Full little think'st thou of thy joy that's coming,
The sweet, sweet joy, full little of the kisses,
But those unthought of things come ever happiest.
How soft the Rogue feels! O ye little Villain,
Ye delicate coy Thief, how I shall thrum ye!
Your 'fy away, good servant, as you are a Gentleman.'

MARY
Prithee leave laughing.

THOMAS
Out upon ye, Thomas,
What do you mean to do? I'll call the house up.
O God, I am sure ye will not, shall not serve ye,
For up ye go now and ye were my father.

MAID
Your courage will be cool'd anon.

THOMAS
If it do I'll hang for't,
Yet I'le be quartered here first.

DOROTHEA
O fierce Villain.

MARY
What would he do indeed, Doll?

DOROTHEA
You had best try him.

THOMAS
I'll kiss thee ere I come to bed, sweet Mary.

MARY
Prithee leave laughing.

DOROTHEA
O for gentle Nicholas.

THOMAS
And view that stormy face that has so thundred me,
A coldness crept over't now? by your leave, candle,
And next door by yours too, so, a pretty, pretty,
Shall I now look upon ye? by this light it moves me.

MARY
Much good may it do you, Sir.

THOMAS
Holy Saints defend me,
The Devil, Devil, Devil, O the Devil.

MARY & DOROTHEA
Ha, ha, ha, ha, the Devil, O the Devil.

THOMAS

I am abus'd most damnedly, most beastly,
Yet if it be a she-Devil; but the house is up,
And here's no staying longer in this Cassock.
Woman, I here disclaim thee; and in vengeance
I'll marry with that Devil, but I'll vex thee.

MARY
By'r Lady, but you shall not, Sir, I'll watch ye.

THOMAS
Plague o' your Spanish leather hide: I'll waken ye;
Devil good night: good night, good Devil.

MOOR
Oh.

THOMAS
Roar again, Devil, roar again.

[Exit **THOMAS**.

MOOR
Oh, O, Sir.

MARY
Open the doors before him; let him vanish:
Now, let him come again, I'll use him kinder.
How now Wench?

MOOR
'Pray lye here your self next, Mistress,
And entertain your sweet-heart.

MARY
What said he to thee?

MOOR
I had a soft Bed, and I slept out all
But his kind farewel: ye may bake me now,
For o' my conscience, he has made me Venison.

MARY
Alas poor Kate: I'll give thee a new Petticoat.

DOROTHEA
And I a Wastecoat, wench.

MARY

Draw in the Bed, Maids,
And see it made again; put fresh sheets on too,
For Doll and I; come Wench, let's laugh an hour now.
To morrow, early, will we see young Cellide,
They say she has taken a Sanctuary; Love and they
Are thick sown, but come up so full of thistles.

DOROTHEA
They must needs, Mall, for 'tis a pricking age grown,
Prithee to bed, for I am monstrous sleepy.

MARY
A match, but art not thou thy Brother?

DOROTHEA
I would I were, Wench,
You should hear further.

MARY
Come, no more of that, Doll.

[Exeunt.

SCÆNA SECUNDA

Enter **HYLAS** and **THOMAS**.

HYLAS
I heard the doors clap; now, and't be thy will, wench.
By th' Mass she comes; you are surely met fair Gentlewoman,
I take it, Mistress Doll Sebastians Daughter.

THOMAS
I take right, Sir; Hylas, are you ferretting?
I'll fit you with a penny-worth presently.

HYLAS
How dare you walk so late, sweet, so weak guarded?

THOMAS
'Faith Sir, I do no harm, nor none I look for,
Yet I am glad I have met so good a Gentleman,
Against all chances; for though I never knew ye,
Yet I have heard much good spoke of ye.

HYLAS

Hark ye,
What if a man should kiss ye?

THOMAS
That's no harm, Sir;
'Pray God he 'scapes my Beard, there lies the mischief.

HYLAS
Her lips are monstrous rugged, but that surely
Is but the sharpness of the weather; hark ye once more,
And in your ear, sweet Mistress, for ye are so,
And ever shall be from this hour: I have vow'd it.

[Enter **SEBASTIAN** and **LAUNCELOT**.

SEBASTIAN
Why, that's my daughter, Rogue, dost thou not see her
Kissing that fellow there, there in that corner?

LAUNCELOT
Kissing?

SEBASTIAN
Now, now, now they agree o'th' match too.

THOMAS
Nay then you love me not.

HYLAS
By this white hand, Doll.

THOMAS
I must confess I have long desir'd your sight, Sir.

LAUNCELOT
Why, there's the Boots still, Sir.

SEBASTIAN
Hang Boots, Sir,
Why, they'll wear Breeches too.

THOMAS
Dishonest me?
Not for the World.

SEBASTIAN
Why, now they kiss again, there
I knew 'twas she, and that her crafty stealing

Out the back way must needs have such a meaning.

LAUNCELOT
I am at my small wits ends.

THOMAS
If ye mean honourably.

LAUNCELOT
Did she ne'r beat ye before, Sir?

SEBASTIAN
Why dost thou follow me?
Thou Rascal, Slave, hast thou not twice abus'd me?
Hast thou not spoil'd the Boy? by thine own Covenant,
Wouldst thou not now be hang'd?

LAUNCELOT
I think I would, Sir,
But you are so impatient; does not this shew, Sir,
(I do beseech ye speak, and speak with judgment,
And let the case be equally consider'd)
Far braver in your Daughter? in a Son now,
'Tis nothing, of no mark; every man does it,
But to beget a Daughter, a man maiden,
That reaches at these high exploits, is admirable;
Nay, she goes far beyond him; for when durst he,
But when he was drunk, do any thing to speak of?
This is Sebastian truly.

SEBASTIAN
Thou sayest right, Launce,
And there's my hand once more.

THOMAS
Not without Marriage.

SEBASTIAN
Didst thou hear that?

LAUNCELOT
I think she spoke of Marriage.

SEBASTIAN
And he shall marry her, for it seems she likes him,
And their first Boy shall be my heir.

LAUNCELOT

I, marry,
Now ye go right to work.

THOMAS
Fye, fie, Sir,
Now I have promis'd ye this night to marry,
Would ye be so intemperate? are ye a Gentleman?

HYLAS
I have no maw to marriage, yet this Rascal
Tempts me extreamly: will ye marry presently?

THOMAS
Get you afore, and stay me at the Chapel,
Close by the Nunnery, there you shall find a night Priest,
Little Sir Hugh, and he can say the Matrimony
Over without Book, for we must have no company,
Nor light, for fear my Father know, which must not yet be;
And then to morrow night.

HYLAS
Nothing to night, Sweet?

THOMAS
No, not a bit, I am sent of business,
About my dowry, Sweet, do not spoil all now,
'Tis of much haste: I can scarce stay the marriage,
Now if you love me, get you gone.

HYLAS
You'll follow?

THOMAS
Within this hour, my sweet Chick.

HYLAS
Kiss.

THOMAS
A Rope kiss ye,
Come, come, I stand o' thorns.

HYLAS
Methinks her mouth still
Is monstrous rough, but they have ways to mend it,
Farewel.

THOMAS

Farewel, I'll fit ye with a wife, Sir.

SEBASTIAN
Come, follow close, I'll see the end she aims at,
And if he be a handsome fellow, Launcelot,
Fiat, 'tis done, and all my 'state is setled.

[Exeunt.

SCÆNA TERTIA

Enter **ABBESS**, **CELLIDE** and **NUNS**.

ABBESS
Come to your Mattins Maids; these early hours
My gentle Daughter, will disturb a while
Your fair eyes, nurtur'd in ease.

CELLIDE
No, vertuous Mother,
'Tis for my holy health, to purchase which,
They shall forget the Child of ease, soft slumbers.
O my afflicted heart, how thou art tortur'd!
And Love, how like a Tyrant thou reign'st in me,
Commanding and forbidding at one instant;
Why came I hither, that desire to have
Only all liberty to make me happy?
Why did'st thou bring that young man home, O Valentine,
That vertuous Youth? why didst thou speak his goodness
In such a phrase, as if all tongues, all praises
Were made for him? O fond and ignorant!
Why didst thou foster my affection
Till it grew up to know no other Father,
And then betray it?

ABBESS
Can ye sing?

CELLIDE
Yes, Mother,
My sorrows only.

ABBESS
Be gone, and to the Quire then.

[Exeunt.

[Musick singing.

Enter **MICHAEL** and **SERVANT** and **FRANCIS**.

MICHAEL
Hast thou enquir'd him out?

SERVANT
He's not at home, Sir,
His Sister thinks he's gone to th' Nunnery.

MICHAEL
Most likely; I'll away, an hour hence, Sirrah,
Come you along with this young Gentleman,
Do him all service, and fair office.

SERVANT
Yes Sir.

[Exeunt.

Enter **HYLAS** and **SAM**.

SAM
Where hast thou been, man?

HYLAS
Is there ne'r a shop open?
I'll give thee a pair of Gloves, Sam.

SAM
What's the matter?

HYLAS
What dost thou think?

SAM
Thou art not married?

HYLAS
By th' mass but I am, all to be married,
I am i'th' order now, Sam.

SAM
To whom prithee?
I thought there was some such trick in't, you stole from me,
But who, for Heavens sake?

HYLAS
Ev'n the sweetest woman,
The rarest Woman, Samuel, and the lustiest,
But wondrous honest, honest as the ice, Boy,
Not a bit before hand, for my life, Sirrah,
And of a lusty kindred.

SAM
But who, Hylas?

HYLAS
The young Gentleman and I are like to be friends again,
The fates will have it so.

SAM
Who, Monsieur Thomas?

HYLAS
All wrongs forgot.

SAM
O now I smell ye, Hylas;
Does he know of it?

HYLAS
No there's the trick I owe him;
'Tis done, Boy, we are fast 'faith, my Youth now
Shall know I am aforehand, for his qualities.

SAM
Is there no trick in't?

HYLAS
None, but up and ride, Boy:
I have made no Joynture neither, there I have paid him.

SAM
She's a brave wench.

HYLAS
She shall be as I'll use her,
And if she anger me, all his abuses
I'll clap upon her Cassock.

SAM
Take heed, Hylas.

HYLAS
'Tis past that, Sam, come, I must meet her presently,
And now shalt see me a most glorious Husband.

[Exeunt.

SCÆNA SEXTA

Enter **DOROTHEA, MARY, VALENTINE**.

DOROTHEA
In troth, Sir, you never spoke to me.

VALENTINE
Can ye forget me?
Did not you promise all your help and cunning
In my behalf, but for one hour to see her,
Did you not swear it? by this hand, no strictness
Nor rule this house holds, shall by me be broken.

DOROTHEA
I saw ye not these two days.

VALENTINE
Do not wrong me,
I met ye, by my life, just as you entred
This gentle Ladies Lodge, last night, thus suited
About eleven a clock.

DOROTHEA
'Tis true, I was there,
But that I saw or spoke to you.

MARY
I have found it,
Your Brother Thomas, Doll.

DOROTHEA

Pray Sir, be satisfi'd,
And wherein I can do you good, command me.
What a mad fool is this! stay here a while, Sir,
Whilst we walk in, and make your peace.

[Exit.

[Enter **ABBESS**.

VALENTINE
I thank ye.

[Squeak within.

Ab. Why, what's the matter there among these maids?
Now benedicite, have ye got the breeze there?
Give me my holy sprinkle.

[Enter Two **NUNS**.

1ST NUN
O Madam, there's a strange thing like a Gentlewoman,
Like Mistress Dorothea, I think the fiend
Crept into th' Nunnery we know not which way,
Plays revel rout among us.

ABBESS
Give me my holy water-pot.

1ST NUN
Here, Madam.

ABBESS
Spirit of earth or air, I do conjure thee,

[Squeak within.

Of water or of fire.

1ST NUN
Hark Madam, hark.

ABBESS
Be thou Ghost that cannot rest,
Or a shadow of the blest,
Be thou black, or white, or green,
Be thou heard, or to be seen.

[Enter **THOMAS** and **CELLIDE**.

2ND NUN

2ND NUN
It comes, it comes.

CELLIDE
What are ye? speak, speak gently,
And next, what would ye with me?

THOMAS
Any thing you'l let me.

CELLIDE
You are no Woman certain.

THOMAS
Nor you no Nun, nor shall not be.

CELLIDE
What make ye here?

THOMAS
I am a holy Fryer.

ABBESS
Is this the Spirit?

THOMAS
Nothing but spirit Aunt.

ABBESS
Now out upon thee.

THOMAS
Peace, or I'le conjure too, Aunt.

ABBESS
Why come you thus?

THOMAS
That's all one, here's my purpose:
Out with this Nun, she is too handsome for ye,
I'le tell thee, Aunt, and I speak it with tears to thee,
If thou keepst her here, as yet I hope thou art wiser,
Mark but the mischief follows.

ABBESS
She is a Votress.

THOMAS
Let her be what she will, she will undo thee,
Let her but one hour out, as I direct ye,
Or have among your Nuns again.

ABBESS
You have no project
But fair and honest?

THOMAS
As thine eyes, sweet Abbess.

ABBESS
I will be rul'd then.

THOMAS
Thus then and perswade her,
But do not juggle with me, if ye do Aunt.

ABBESS
I must be there my self.

THOMAS
Away and fit her.

ABBESS
Come Daughter, you must now be rul'd, or never.

CELLIDE
I must obey your will.

ABBESS
That's my good Daughter.

[Exeunt.

SCÆNA SEPTIMA

Enter **DOROTHEA** and **MARY**.

MARY
What a coyle has this fellow kept i'th' Nunnery,
Sure he has run the Abbess out of her wits.

Do. Out of the Nunnery I think, for we can neither see her,

Nor the young Cellide.

MARY
Pray Heavens he be not teasing.

DOROTHEA
Nay you may thank your self, 'twas your own structures.

[Enter **HYLAS** and **SAM**.

SAM
Why there's the Gentlewoman.

HYLAS
Mass 'tis she indeed;
How smart the pretty Thief looks! 'morrow Mistress.

DOROTHEA
Good morrow to you, Sir.

SAM
How strange she bears it!

HYLAS
Maids must do so, at first.

DOROTHEA
Would ye ought with us, Gentlemen?

HYLAS
Yes marry would I,
A little with your Ladyship.

DOROTHEA
Your will, Sir.

HYLAS
Doll, I would have ye presently prepare your self
And those things you would have with you,
For my house is ready.

DOROTHEA
How, Sir?

HYLAS
And this night not to fail, you must come to me,
My friends will all be there too: for Trunks, and those things,
And houshold-stuff, and cloaths you would have carried,

To morrow, or the next day, I'le take order:
Only what mony you have, bring away with ye,
And Jewels.

DOROTHEA
Jewels, Sir?

HYLAS
I, for adornment,
There's a bed up, to play the game in, Dorothea:
And now come kiss me heartily.

DOROTHEA
Who are you?

HYLAS
This Lady shall be welcome too.

MARY
To what, Sir?

HYLAS
Your neighbour can resolve ye.

DOROTHEA
The man's foolish,
Sir, you look soberly: who is this fellow,
And where's his business?

SAM
By Heaven, thou art abus'd still.

HYLAS
It may be so: Come, ye may speak now boldly,
There's none but friends, Wench.

DOROTHEA
Came ye out of Bedlam?
Alas, 'tis ill, Sir, that ye suffer him
To walk in th' open Air thus: 'twill undo him.
A pretty handsome Gentleman: great pity.

SAM
Let me not live more if thou be'st not cozen'd.

HYLAS
Are not you my Wife? did not I marry you last night
At St Michaels Chapel?

DOROTHEA
Did not I say he was mad?

HYLAS
Are not you Mistress Dorothea, Thomas's Sister?

MARY
There he speaks sence, but I'le assure ye, Gentleman,
I think no Wife of yours: at what hour was it?

HYLAS
'S pretious; you'l make me mad; did not the Priest,
Sir Hugh, that you appointed, about twelve a Clock
Tye our hands fast? did not you swear you lov'd me?
Did not I court ye, coming from this Gentlewomans?

MARY
Good Sir, go sleep: for if I credit have,
She was in my arms then, abed.

SAM
I told ye.

HYLAS
Be not so confident.

DOROTHEA
By th' mass, she must, Sir;
For I'le no Husband here, before I know him:
And so good morrow to ye: Come, let's go seek 'em.

SAM
I told ye what ye had done.

HYLAS
Is the Devil stirring?
Well, go with me; for now I will be married.

[Exeunt.

SCÆNA OCTAVIA

Enter **MICHAEL**, **VALENTINE** and **ALICE**.

MICHAEL

I have brought him back again.

VALENTINE
You have done a friendship,
Worthy the love you bear me.

MICHAEL
Would he had so too.

VALENTINE
O he's a worthy young man.

MICHAEL
When all's try'd,
I fear you'll change your faith: bring in the Gentleman.

[Enter **FRANCIS**, **SERVANT**, **ABBESS** and **CELLIDE**, severally.

VALENTINE
My happy Mistress too! now Fortune help me,
And all you Stars that govern chast desires
Shine fair, and lovely.

ABBESS
But one hour, dear Daughter,
To hear your Guardian, what he can deliver
In Loves defence, and his: and then your pleasure.

CELLIDE
Though much unwilling, you have made me yield,
More for his sake I see: how full of sorrow
Sweet catching sorrow, he appears! O love,
That thou but knew'st to heal, as well as hurt us.

MICHAEL
Be rul'd by me: I see her eye fast on him:
And what ye heard, believe, for 'tis so certain
He neither dar'd, nor must oppose my evidence;
And be you wise, young Lady, and believe too,
This man you love, Sir?

VALENTINE
As I love my soul, Sir.

MICHAEL
This man you put into a free possession
Of what his wants could ask: or your self render?

VALENTINE
And shall do still.

MICHAEL
Nothing was barr'd his liberty
But this fair Maid; that friendship first was broken,
And you, and she abus'd; next, (to my sorrow
So fair a form should hide so dark intentions)
He hath himself confess'd (my purpose being
Only to stop his journey, by that policy
Of laying Felony to his charge, to fright the Sailers)
Divers abuses done, Thefts often practis'd,
Monyes, and Jewels too, and those no trifles.

CELLIDE
O where have I bestrew'd my faith! in neither!
Let's in for ever now, there is vertue.

MICHAEL
Nay do not wonder at it, he shall say it:
Are ye not guilty thus?

FRANCIS
Yes: O my Fortune!

MICHAEL
To give a proof I speak not enviously,
Look here; do you know these Jewels?

CELLIDE
In, good Mother.

[Enter **THOMAS**, **DOROTHEA** and **MARY**: then **SEBASTIAN** and **LAUNCELOT**.

VALENTINE
These Jewels I have known.

DOROTHEA
You have made brave sport.

THOMAS
I'le make more, if I live Wench,
Nay do not look on me; I care not for ye.

LAUNCELOT
Do you see now plain? that's Mistris Dorothea,
And that's his Mistris.

SEBASTIAN
Peace, let my joy work easily,
Ha, boy! art there my boy? mine own boy, Tom, boy,
Home Lance, and strike a fresh piece of Wine, the Town's ours.

VALENTINE
Sure, I have known these Jewels.

ALICE
They are they, certain.

VALENTINE
Good Heaven, that they were.

ALICE
I'le pawn my life on't,
And this is he; come hither Mistris Dorothea,
And Mistris Mary: who does that face look like;
And view my Brother well?

DOROTHEA
In truth like him.

MARY
Upon my troth exceeding like.

MICHAEL
Beshrew me,
But much, and main resemblance, both of face
And lineaments of body: now Heaven grant it.

ALICE
My Brother's full of passion, I'le speak to him.
Now, as you are a Gentleman, resolve me,
Where did you get these Jewels?

FRANCIS
Now I'le tell ye,
Because blind fortune yet may make me happy,
Of whom I had 'em I have never heard yet,
But from my infancy, upon this arm
I ever wore 'em.

ALICE
'Tis Francisco, Brother,
By Heaven I ty'd 'em on: a little more, Sir,
A little, little more, what parents have ye?

FRANCIS
None,
That I know yet: the more my stubborn fortune,
But as I heard a Merchant say that bred me,
Who, to my more affliction, dyed a poor man,
When I reach'd eighteen years.

ALICE
What said that Merchant?

FRANCIS
He said, an infant, in the Genoway Galleys,
But from what place he never could direct me,
I was taken in a Sea-fight, and from a Mariner,
Out of his manly pity he redeem'd me.
He told me of a Nurse that waited on me,
But she, poor soul, he said was killed.
A Letter too I had enclos'd within me,
To one Castruccio a Venetian Merchant,
To bring me up: the man, when years allow'd me,
And want of friends compell'd, I sought, but found him
Long dead before, and all my hopes gone with him.
The Wars was my retreat then, and my travel
In which I found this Gentlemans free bounty,
For which Heaven recompenc'd him: now ye have all.

VALENTINE
And all the worldly bliss that Heaven can send me,
And all my prayers and thanks.

ALICE
Down o' your knees, Sir,
For now you have found a Father, and that Father
That will not venture ye again in Galleys.

MICHAEL
'Tis true, believe her, Sir, and we all joy with ye.

VALENTINE
My best friend still: my dearest: now Heaven bless thee,
And make me worthy of this benefit.
Now my best Mistress.

CELLIDE
Now Sir, I come to ye.

ABBESS
No, no, let's in Wench.

CELLIDE
Not for the world, now, Mother,
And thus, Sir, all my service I pay to you,
And all my love to him.

VALENTINE
And may it prosper,
Take her Francisco: now no more young Callidon,
And love her dearly, for thy Father does so.

FRANCIS
May all hate seek me else, and thus I seal it.

VALENTINE
Nothing but mirth now, friends.

[Enter **HYLAS** and **SAM**.

HYLAS
Nay, I will find him.

SAM
What do all these here?

THOMAS
You are a trusty Husband,
And a hot lover too.

HYLAS
Nay then, good morrow,
Now I perceive the Knavery.

SAM
I still told ye.

THOMAS
Stay, or I'le make ye stay: come hither, Sister.

VALENTINE
Why how now Mistris Thomas?

THOMAS
Peace a little,
Thou would'st fain have a Wife?

HYLAS
Not I, by no means.

THOMAS
Thou shalt have a wife, and a fruitful wife, for I find,
Hylas,
That I shall never be able to bring thee Children.

SEBASTIAN
A notable brave boy.

HYLAS
I am very well, Sir.

THOMAS
Thou shalt be better, Hylas, thou hast 7 hundred pound a year,
And thou shalt make her 3 hundred joynture.

HYLAS
No.

THOMAS
Thou shalt boy, and shalt bestow
Two hundred pound in Cloaths, look on her,
A delicate lusty wench, she has fifteen hundred,
And feasible: strike hands, or I'le strike first.

DOROTHEA
You'l let me like?

MARY
He's a good handsome fellow,
Play not the fool.

THOMAS
Strike, Brother Hylas, quickly.

HYLAS
If you can love me, well.

DOROTHEA
If you can please me.

THOMAS
Try that out soon, I say, my Brother Hylas.

SAM
Take her, and use her well, she's a brave Gentlewoman.

HYLAS

You must allow me another Mistriss.

DOROTHEA
Then you must allow me another Servant.

HYLAS
Well, let's together then, a lusty kindred.

SEBASTIAN
I'le give thee five hundred pound more for that word.

MARY
Now Sir, for you and I to make the feast full.

THOMAS
No, not a bit, you are a vertuous Lady,
And love to live in contemplation.

MARY
Come fool, I am friends now.

THOMAS
The fool shall not ride ye,
There lye my Woman, now my man again,
And now for travel once more.

SEBASTIAN
I'le barr that first.

MARY
And I next.

THOMAS
Hold your self contented: for I say I will travel,
And so long I will travel, till I find a Father
That I never knew, and a Wife that I never look'd for,
And a state without expectation,
So rest you merry Gentlemen.

MARY
You shall not,
Upon my faith, I love you now extreamly,
And now I'le kiss ye.

THOMAS
This will not do it, Mistress.

MARY

Why when we are married, we'l do more.

SEBASTIAN
There's all Boy,
The keyes of all I have, come, let's be merry,
For now I see thou art right.

THOMAS
Shall we to Church straight?

VALENTINE
Now presently, and there with nuptial
The holy Priest shall make ye happy all.

THOMAS
Away then, fair afore.

[Exeunt.

TO THE NOBLE HONOURER OF THE Dead Author's Works and Memory, Master CHARLES COTTON.

SIR,

My directing of this piece unto you, renders me obvious to many censures, which I would willingly prevent by declaring mine own and your right thereto. Mine was the fortune to be made the unworthy preserver of it; yours is the worthy opinion you have of the Author and his Poems; neither can it easily be determined, whether your affection to them hath made you (by observing) more able to judge of them, than your ability to judge of them hath made you to affect them, deservedly, not partially. In this presumptuous act of mine, I express my twofold zeal; to him and your noble self, who have built him a more honourable monument in that fair opinion you have of him, than any inscription subject to the wearing of time can be. You will find him in this Poem as active as in others, to many of which, the dull apprehensions of former times gave but slender allowance, from malitious custom more than reason: yet they have since by your candid self and others, been clearly vindicated. You shall oblige by your acceptance of this acknowledgment (which is the best I can render you, mine own weak la[b]ours being too unworthy your judicious perusal) him that is ambitious to be known.

Your most humble Servant,

John Fletcher – A Short Biography

John Fletcher was born in December, 1579 in Rye, Sussex. He was baptised on December 20th.

As can be imagined details of much of his life and career have not survived and, accordingly, only a very brief indication of his life and works can be given.

His father, Richard Fletcher, was a successful and rather ambitious cleric. From being the Dean of Peterborough he moved on to become the Bishop of Bristol, Bishop of Worcester and finally, shortly before his death, the Bishop of London. He was also the chaplain to Queen Elizabeth.

When he was Dean of Peterborough, Richard Fletcher, witnessed the execution of Mary, Queen of Scots. It was said he "knelt down on the scaffold steps and started to pray out loud and at length, in a prolonged and rhetorical style, as though determined to force his way into the pages of history". He cried out at her death, "So perish all the Queen's enemies!" All very dramatic but the family did have strong links to the Arts.

Young Fletcher appears at the very young age of eleven to have entered Corpus Christi College at Cambridge University in 1591. There are no records that he ever took a degree but there is some small evidence that he was being prepared for a career in the church.

However what is clear is that this was soon abandoned as he joined the stream of people who would leave University and decamp to the more bohemian life of commercial theatre in London.

Unfortunately his father fell out with Queen Elizabeth but appears to have been on his way to rehabilitation before his death in 1596. At his death he was, however, mired in debt.

The upbringing of the now teenage Fletcher and his seven siblings now passed to his paternal uncle, the poet and minor official Giles Fletcher. Giles, who had the patronage of the Earl of Essex may have been a liability rather than an advantage to the young Fletcher. With Essex involved in the failed rebellion against Elizabeth Giles was also tainted by association.

By 1606 John Fletcher appears to have equipped himself with the talents to become a playwright. Initially this appears to have been for the Children of the Queen's Revels, then performing at the Blackfriars Theatre.

Commendatory verses by Richard Brome in the Beaumont and Fletcher 1647 folio place Fletcher in the company of Ben Jonson, although it is not known when this friendship began. Jonson, of course, was a leviathan of English Literature, so admired that many of his literary friends and colleagues were simply known as 'Sons of Ben'. Fletcher's frequent early collaborator, Francis Beaumont, was also a friend of Jonson's.

Fletcher's early career was marked by one significant failure; The Faithful Shepherdess, his adaptation of Giovanni Battista Guarini's Il Pastor Fido, which was performed by the Blackfriars Children in 1608. In the preface to the printed edition of his play, Fletcher explained the failure as due to his audience's faulty expectations. They expected a pastoral tragicomedy to feature dances, comedy, and murder, with the shepherds presented in conventional stereotypes – as Fletcher put it, wearing "gray cloaks, with curtailed dogs in strings." Fletcher's preface is however best known for its pithy definition of tragicomedy: "A tragicomedy is not so called in respect of mirth and killing, but in respect it wants [i.e., lacks] deaths, which is enough to make it no tragedy; yet brings some near it, which is enough to make it no comedy." A comedy, he went on to say, must be "a representation of familiar people." His preface is critical of drama that features characters whose action violates nature.

In that case, Fletcher appears to have been developing a new style faster than audiences could comprehend. By 1609, however, he had found his stride. With Beaumont, he wrote Philaster, which became a hit for the King's Men and began a profitable association between Fletcher and that company. Philaster appears also to have begun a trend for tragicomedy. Fletcher's influence has also been said to have inspired some features of Shakespeare's late romances, and certainly his influence on the tragicomic work of other playwrights is even more marked.

By the middle of the 1610s, Fletcher's plays had achieved a popularity that rivalled Shakespeare's and cemented the pre-eminence of the King's Men in Jacobean London. After Beaumont's retirement, necessitated by ill-health, and then his early death in 1616, Fletcher continued working, both singly and in collaboration, until his death in 1625. By that time, he had produced, or had been credited with, close to fifty plays. This body of work remained a major part of the King's Men's repertory until the closing of the theatres in 1642 due to the Civil War.

At the beginning of his career Fletcher's most important collaborator was Francis Beaumont. The two wrote together for close to a decade, first for the Children of the Queen's Revels, and then for the King's Men. According to an anecdote transmitted or invented by John Aubrey, they also lived together in Bankside, sharing clothes and having "one wench in the house between them." This domestic arrangement, if it existed, was ended by Beaumont's marriage in 1613, and their dramatic partnership ended after Beaumont fell ill, probably of a stroke, that same year.

At this point Fletcher had written many plays with Beaumont and several others on his own. He seems to have been regarded as quite a talent although it should be remembered that playwrights were required to be prolific, to easily work with other collaborators and to produce work of quality and commercial appeal very quickly.

The King's Men, run by Philip Henslowe, was the most prestigious of the theatre companies and Fletcher now had an increasingly close association with it.

Fletcher collaborated with Shakespeare on Henry VIII, The Two Noble Kinsmen, and the now lost Cardenio, which some scholars say was the basis for Lewis Theobald's play Double Falsehood. (Theobald is regarded as one of the best Shakespearean editors. Whether his play is based on Cardenio or on some other is not absolutely known although Theobald certainly promoted it as his revision of the lost Shakespeare/Fletcher play.)

A play that Fletcher also wrote by himself at this time, The Woman's Prize or the Tamer Tamed, is also regarded as a sequel to The Taming of the Shrew.

In 1616, with the death of Shakespeare, Fletcher now appears to have entered into an enhanced arrangement with the King's Men on very similar terms to Shakespeare's. Fletcher would now write exclusively for the King's Men until his own death almost a decade later.

As well as continuing his solo productions Fletcher was still collaborating with other playwrights, mainly Philip Massinger, who, in turn, would succeed him as the in-house playwright for the King's Men.

Fletcher's popularity continued throughout his life; indeed during the winter of 1621, he had three of his plays performed at court. His mastery is most notable in two dramatic types; tragicomedy and the comedy of manners.

John Fletcher died in 1625, it is thought of bubonic plague which, at the time, was undergoing further outbreaks.

He seems to have been buried in what is now Southwark Cathedral, although a precise location is not known. There is much made of an anecdote that Fletcher and Massinger (who died in 1640) share the same grave but it is more likely that both are buried within a few yards of each other and that the stone markers in the floor have confused the issue. One is marked 'Edmond Shakespeare 1607' and the other 'John Fletcher 1625' refers to Shakespeare's younger brother and the playwright. The churchyards were, more often than not, completely over-crowded and breeding grounds for disease. Precise record keeping was not a practiced skill.

During the later Commonwealth, many of the playwright's best-known scenes were kept alive as drolls. These were brief performances, usually condensed into one or two scenes and with the addition of music or song to satisfy the taste for plays while the theatres were closed under the Puritans. At the re-opening of the theatres in 1660, the plays in the Fletcher canon, in original form or revised, were by far the most common productions on the English stage. The most frequently revived plays suggest the developing taste for comedies of manners. Among the tragedies, The Maid's Tragedy and, especially, Rollo Duke of Normandy held the stage. Four tragicomedies (A King and No King, The Humorous Lieutenant, Philaster, and The Island Princess) were popular, perhaps in part for their similarity to and foreshadowing of heroic drama. Four comedies (Rule a Wife And Have a Wife, The Chances, Beggars' Bush, and especially The Scornful Lady) were also stage mainstays.

Despite his popularity, and it appears he was held in higher regard than Shakespeare at this time, his works steadily lost ground to those of Shakespeare and to new productions from other playwrights.

Since then Fletcher has increasingly become a subject only for occasional revivals and for specialists. Fletcher and his collaborators have been the subject of important bibliographic and critical studies, but the plays have been revived only infrequently.

Due to the frequent collaborations between all manner of playwrights, and the revisions carried out in later years, having a settled list of authorship to any given set of plays can be problematic. The works of Fletcher and others of this period most definitely fall into this category. It is as well to take into account that during this period theatres were quite often closed either due to outbreaks of the plague or to the prevailing political and moral climate. Printers, anxious to provide materials that would sell, were not above changing a name or two to enhance sales.

Although Fletcher collaborated most often with Beaumont and Massinger, it is believed that Massinger revised many of the plays some time after their original production. Other collaborators including Nathan Field, William Shakespeare, William Rowley and others also can be seen distinctly in Fletchers' works. Many modern scholars point out that Fletcher had many particular mannerisms but other playwrights would also duplicate these at times so allocating exact contributions of anyone to a play is somewhat of a detective case in many instances. However from the original folio printings or licensing via the Master of the Revels (the statutory licensing authority to approve and censor plays as well a hand in publication and printing of theatrical materials) as well as contemporary notes a fairly precise bibliography of the works can be given with only a few plays lacking substantial authority and provenance.

John Fletcher – A Concise Bibliography

This bibliography gives the most likely date of writing together with when published, revised or licensed by the Master or the Revels (This position within the royal household was originally for royal festivities, ie revels, and later to oversee stage censorship, until this function was transferred to the Lord Chamberlain in 1624).

Solo Plays
The Faithful Shepherdess, pastoral (written 1608–9; printed 1609)
The Tragedy of Valentinian, tragedy (1610–14; 1647)
Monsieur Thomas, comedy (c. 1610–16; 1639)
The Woman's Prize, or The Tamer Tamed, comedy (c. 1611; 1647)
Bonduca, tragedy (1611–14; 1647)
The Chances, comedy (c. 1613–25; 1647)
Wit Without Money, comedy (c. 1614; 1639)
The Mad Lover, tragicomedy (acted 5 January 1617; 1647)
The Loyal Subject, tragicomedy (licensed 16 November 1618; revised 1633; 1647)
The Humorous Lieutenant, tragicomedy (c. 1619; 1647)
Women Pleased, tragicomedy (c. 1619–23; 1647)
The Island Princess, tragicomedy (c. 1620; 1647)
The Wild Goose Chase, comedy (c. 1621; 1652)
The Pilgrim, comedy (c. 1621; 1647)
A Wife for a Month, tragicomedy (licensed 27 May 1624; 1647)
Rule a Wife and Have a Wife, comedy (licensed 19 October 1624; 1640)

Collaborations

With Francis Beaumont
The Woman Hater, comedy (1606; 1607)
Cupid's Revenge, tragedy (c. 1607–12; 1615)
Philaster, or Love Lies a-Bleeding, tragicomedy (c. 1609; 1620)
The Maid's Tragedy, Tragedy (c. 1609; 1619)
A King and No King, tragicomedy (1611; 1619)
The Captain, comedy (c. 1609–12; 1647)
The Scornful Lady, comedy (c. 1613; 1616)
Love's Pilgrimage, tragicomedy (c. 1615–16; 1647)
The Noble Gentleman, comedy (c. 1613; licensed 3 February 1626; 1647)

With Francis Beaumont & Philip Massinger
Thierry & Theodoret, tragedy (c. 1607; 1621)
The Coxcomb, comedy (c. 1608–10; 1647)
Beggars' Bush, comedy (c. 1612–13; revised 1622; 1647)

Love's Cure, comedy (c. 1612–13; revised 1625; 1647)

Sir John van Olden Barnavelt, tragedy (August 1619; MS)
The Little French Lawyer, comedy (c. 1619–23; 1647)
A Very Woman, tragicomedy (c. 1619–22; licensed 6 June 1634; 1655)
The Custom of the Country, comedy (c. 1619–23; 1647)
The Double Marriage, tragedy (c. 1619–23; 1647)
The False One, history (c. 1619–23; 1647)
The Prophetess, tragicomedy (licensed 14 May 1622; 1647)
The Sea Voyage, comedy (licensed 22 June 1622; 1647)
The Spanish Curate, comedy (licensed 24 October 1622; 1647)
The Lovers' Progress or The Wandering Lovers, tragicomedy (licensed 6 December 1623; rev 1634; 1647)
The Elder Brother, comedy (c. 1625; 1637)

The Honest Man's Fortune, tragicomedy (1613; 1647)
The Queen of Corinth, tragicomedy (c. 1616–18; 1647)
The Knight of Malta, tragicomedy (c. 1619; 1647)

Henry VIII, history (c. 1613; 1623)
The Two Noble Kinsmen, tragicomedy (c. 1613; 1634)
Cardenio, tragicomedy (c. 1613)

Wit at Several Weapons, comedy (c. 1610–20; 1647)

The Maid in the Mill (licensed 29 August 1623; 1647).

Four Plays, or Moral Representations, in One, morality (c. 1608–13; 1647)

Rollo Duke of Normandy, or The Bloody Brother, tragedy (c. 1617; revised 1627–30; 1639)

The Night Walker, or The Little Thief, comedy (c. 1611; 1640)
The Coronation c. 1635

The Nice Valour, or The Passionate Madman, comedy (c. 1615–25; 1647)
The Laws of Candy, tragicomedy (c. 1619–23; 1647)
The Fair Maid of the Inn, comedy (licensed 22 January 1626; 1647)
The Faithful Friends, tragicomedy (registered 29 June 1660; MS.)

The Nice Valour is possibly by Fletcher revised by Thomas Middleton;

The Fair Maid of the Inn is perhaps a play by Massinger, John Ford, and John Webster, either with or without Fletcher's involvement.

The Laws of Candy has been variously attributed to Fletcher and to John Ford.

The Night-Walker was a Fletcher original, with additions by Shirley for a 1639 production.

Even now there is not absolute certainty on several of the plays. The first Beaumont & Fletcher folio of 1647 contained 35 plays and the second folio of 1679 added a further 18. In total 53 plays.

The first folio included The Masque of the Inner Temple and Gray's Inn (1613), and the second The Knight of the Burning Pestle (1607), widely considered Beaumont's solo works, although the latter was in early editions attributed to both writers. Fletcher himself said that Beaumont was attributed so-authorship of many works that belonged solely to Fletcher or to other collaborators.

One play in the canon, Sir John Van Olden Barnavelt, existed in manuscript and was not published till 1883.

www.ingramcontent.com/pod-product-compliance
Lightning Source LLC
Chambersburg PA
CBHW060313050426
42448CB00009B/1815